GINGER

Ginger

Herb of the
Year 2023

INTERNATIONAL HERB ASSOCIATION

Kathleen Connole, Editor

International Herb Association

IHA HERB OF THE YEAR

Each year the International Herb Association chooses an **Herb of the Year™** to highlight. The Horticultural Committee evaluates possible choices based on their being outstanding in at least two of the three major categories: culinary, medicinal, and ornamental.

Herb of the Year™ books are published annually by the International Herb Association, P.O. Box 5667 Jacksonville, Florida 32247-5667.

www.iherb.org

This book is intended as an informational guide. The remedies, approaches, and techniques described herein are meant to supplement, and are not to be a substitute for professional medical care or treatment; please consult your healthcare provider.

The International Herb Association is a professional trade organization providing education, service, and development for members engaged in all aspects of the herbal industry.

ISBN: 979-8-9878959-0-0

**Uniting Herb Professionals for Growth
Through Promotion and Education**

The International Herb Association has some of the most dedicated volunteers who keep the organization afloat, giving their time and talents to ensure that IHA continues to share herbal knowledge and connect those in the profession of herbs. We are deeply indebted to the IHA Board of Directors, the IHA Foundation members, and our webmaster. Thanks for all that you do and for caring enough to move us forward!

ACKNOWLEDGEMENTS

For my second year as editor of the Herb of the Year book, I do not think that we could have chosen a more interesting and beneficial herb than Ginger.

I would like to thank all the contributors who responded so enthusiastically with a wonderful variety of topics.

Tina Marie Wilcox, Lucie Day, and Marge Powell provide us with useful, practical details on growing ginger for personal or commercial use in a variety of climates.

Gert Coleman has found fun and fascinating examples of ginger in literature, language, folklore, and poetry, and Karen O'Brien tells of the long and very interesting history and its many uses from ancient times to present.

Our native wild ginger, *Asarum canadense*, is covered by Deborah Hall and Susan Belsinger, so that there will be no confusing *Asarum* with *Zingiber* even though they share the common name "ginger."

Ginger in the Kitchen contains a wide variety of recipes using this spicy rhizome. Susan Belsinger, Gert Coleman, Pat Crocker, Karen England, Donna Frawley, Cooper Murray, Diann Nance, Marge Powell, and Skye Suter provide mouth-watering dishes ranging from sweets to main courses and beverages that not only taste wonderful but may help us stay healthy.

The numerous medicinal uses of ginger are covered extensively by Daniel Gagnon and Dorene Petersen. Carol Little shares her knowledge of ginger as medicine as well. There are lovely recipes for ways to use ginger for health and beauty by Janice Cox.

The photographs of ginger in its many forms, from growing in the garden, cold frame, and containers; to the colorful freshly dug rhizomes, to delicious-looking dishes, have been provided by Susan Belsinger, Lucie Day, Pat Kenny, Karen England, Cooper Murray, Diann Nance, Marge Powell, and Tina Marie Wilcox.

Great admiration goes to our very creative illustrators, Deborah Hall, Pat Kenny, Alicia Mann, and Gail Wood Miller.

Words cannot express adequately the gratitude for the help that was given by Susan Belsinger, Gert Coleman, and Tina Marie Wilcox as second (and third, and fourth, and so on...) readers and editorial advisors with infinite patience.

Many thanks to the incredibly talented Heather Cohen, who was able to execute Susan Belsinger's design vision and create the most beautiful Ginger book cover that we could have imagined.

I would like to thank the IHA Foundation and Board for all that they do to support and promote this very worthwhile organization and the Herb of the Year. I greatly appreciate the Board's encouragement and confidence in my abilities.

Finally, I would like to thank my family members who have cheered me on in this still very new endeavor; especially husband Jeffrey Connole for being my support system and helping in so many little ways to make life easier. Not to mention his frequent baking of gingerbread, as the spicy scent wafts from the kitchen to my upstairs study and makes it somewhat hard to concentrate!

~ Kathleen Connole, Editor

One of the earliest botanical illustrations of *Zingiber officinale*, then known as *Amomum zingiber*.

H.A. Drakestein, Hortus Indicus Malabaricus, 1692. plantillustrations.org

Ginger, *Zingiber officinale* Roscoe

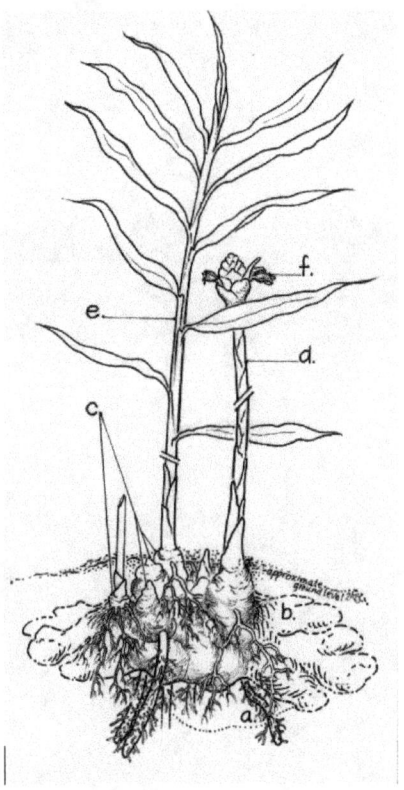

Ginger Illustration by *Pat Kenny*

a. Grandparent rhizome
b. Parent rhizome
c. Baby or annual ginger sprouts
d. Leafless peduncle of blossom spike
e. Aerial shoot or pseudostem of sheathed leaves
f. Inflorescence with bracts and sterile flowers

TABLE OF CONTENTS

Acknowledgements

Ginger in the Kitchen

Freshly dug ginger rhizomes, Harbinger Farm, Myrtle Creek, Oregon.
Susan Belsinger

**Lucie Day in her hoophouse at Harbinger Farm digging
fresh ginger rhizomes from 100-foot row.**
Susan Belsinger

GROWING TROPICAL GINGER IN SOUTHERN OREGON

Lucie Day

In early January 2022, we pre-ordered organic Peruvian yellow ginger rhizomes from Biker Dude of Puna Organics, out of Pahoa, Hawaii (www.hawaiianorganicginger.com), who implement top-notch growing practices, including starting their seed stock from tissue culture so that it is free of pathogens. Our order shipped out freshly dug by the first week of February. When the precious package arrived—15 pounds of gorgeous golden ginger seed (*Zingiber officinale*)—we were able to hold it safely at 70°F for a few days until we had time enough to get them sown.

To initiate the sprouting process, we cut the hands (sections of rhizomes) up into generous finger pieces and laid them out in open flats of fine seedling soil, then covered them with about an inch of topsoil and dampened well.

From there, we made sure to keep them warm (80°F), moist and dark in our germination chamber until they began to emerge, which happened rather sporadically after about two weeks of nothing to note and continued to pop up here and there over the next month. Once we saw the first signs of vegetative growth, we removed the flats from the germ chamber and kept them in the propagation greenhouse at about 70°F with natural light and consistent watering until mid-May when the threat of frost had passed.

When we could rely on the soil temp remaining above 50°F, we transplanted out into our unheated poly-tunnel in the field. We carefully separated the sprouted rhizomes from the seedling flat, spread them out in a single, well-hilled 100-foot row, and buried them 6- to 8-inches deep. A drip irrigation line was tucked in alongside the stalks and buried only lightly under the soil to keep water from running down the slope. Temperature was regulated passively during the day by raising the side walls for ventilation.

Seed rhizomes ready for planting.
Lucie Day

Ginger is a heavy nitrogen feeder, so many applications were applied throughout the growing season. Prior to planting, the beds were prepped with biochar, compost, fishbone meal and pelletized chicken manure. Chicken manure was applied twice more, along with continued hilling in an effort to keep the rhizomes well-covered. Alternating with the top dressings, foliar feedings were also applied, consisting of fish emulsion and kelp. At first, the plants seemingly took a while to catch, but new sprouts continued to emerge, signaling the activity underground—the hands were growing more fingers!—and by late July we had a dense hedgerow of beautiful, lush green bamboo-like stalks, about 2 to 3 feet tall.

100-foot hoophouse, ginger row on left, peppers on right.
Susan Belsinger

A test batch was dug mid-August to see how things were progressing. The rhizomes were colored a buttery yellow with fuchsia pink tips and the scent was nothing short of heavenly! Still, we knew the hands had a bit of fattening up to do, and so we waited patiently for another month before we started digging 10-foot lots at a time to bring with us to the farmers' market.

Since we don't farm in the tropics (but instead at 43 degrees north!), our soil temps don't remain above the safe 50°F zone for the full 10 months that ginger is usually allowed to grow. So our early-harvested ginger crop is referred to as "young", as opposed to the "mature" stock you'll find in the produce section at the grocery store. This means, our young ginger hasn't had the chance to develop that thick, tannish-brown, calloused skin you might be used to painstakingly peeling off. Instead, young ginger's paper-thin skin can be eaten without any toughness or unpleasant texture. The root itself is also much less fibrous, so it's simple to chop with a knife, and the flavor is comparatively mild, bright and even slightly sweet, not at all harsh—you can chew on a nice-sized coin without overwhelming your palate with spice!

The only real "downside" to young ginger is that it does not carry the same shelf-life as the more mature generation. One must take care in keeping it both from drying out or getting too mushy, and ideally use it fresh or preserve it within one month. Thus far, we have found that the best way to store it in fresh form for ultimate longevity is wrapped in a paper towel inside of a plastic bag (which is not sealed shut) in the crisper drawer of the refrigerator. That said, it freezes quite well and pickles even better!

All in all, it was a fantastic first attempt at growing a tropical crop in a temperate climate. It certainly wasn't easy, but we seemed to luck out with our timing and weather, enough so that we gleaned a very decent yield for our investment. We started with 15 pounds of ginger rhizomes and harvested about 250 pounds, after tops were trimmed.

Our 2022 ginger crop success could not have been achieved without the use of greenhouse space for the entirety of its growing process, as well as careful monitoring, but the hard work was well worth it in the end. We plan to use what we learned this year to hopefully grow an even more prolific crop next season. Who knows, we might even try our hand at cultivating turmeric in 2023—stay tuned!

Founded in March 2020 by Matt and **Lucie Day**, *Harbinger Farm is a small-scale produce farm, located in Myrtle Creek, Oregon, which uses only regenerative practices and organic inputs to provide its local community with a reliable source of real, honest food. The temperate climate in Myrtle Creek, Oregon, permits the cultivation of a wide variety of annual row crops on their farm, so that they may bring 70+ different items to market over the course of the growing season. Stewarding their land with thoughtful consideration of the earth's natural cycles while finding their niche within their rural community continues to be a thrilling adventure. Notably, their first attempt at growing ginger in 2022 was such a wonderful success, they have been encouraged to keep it up for years to come!*

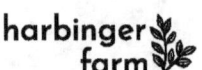

Website: https://www.harbinger-farm.com
email: howdy@harbinger-farm.com
Instagram/Facebook: @harbinger-farm
social: @harbinger-farm

Lucie's hand holding a hand of just-harvested ginger, with the foothills of the Cascade Mountains in the background.

Lucie Day

GROWING GINGER IN THE OZARKS ~ A CONTINUING REAL-LIFE EXPERIMENT

Tina Marie Wilcox

Ginger (*Zingiber officinale*) was just a mysterious, spicy powder in a tin that my mom measured into gingersnap cookie dough until, as an adult, I became a vegetarian. Sometime during my new culinary adventures, a friendly cook introduced me to adding a tablespoon of fresh, finely chopped ginger into stir-fried vegetables. That first time, as the small, moist pieces sizzled in the hot oil in the wok, a pungent, strange heat punched me in the nose. Experiencing the pleasant burning sensation and bold flavor it imparted to the vegetables catapulted me into a deep appreciation for this potent rhizome.

I made my way to the Ozarks. It was early winter, and I was shopping in the produce aisle for Napa cabbage, carrots and cauliflower and found myself gingerly fondling one of the bigger hands of ginger root—it was firm, so full of life force. Being a gardener, I got to wondering, "Reckon this would grow?"

I brought it home. After chopping one of the small fingers protruding from the ginger hand into a vegetable medley, I set upon an experiment to grow this tropical plant in the Ozarks.

I planted the rest of the hand in moist potting soil in a 2-gallon pot. Figuring out which side was up wasn't too difficult. The swollen buds would grow up towards the sun. There were buds on both sides of the rhizome—I just placed the hand flat on the medium and covered it with about an inch of the potting medium. Having not yet met Google, I intuitively decided not to plant it too deeply.

I placed the pot in the greenhouse and moistened the potting medium sporadically during January and February, occasionally sinking my own hand into the medium to find out if the rhizome was still firm. In March the pot was watered about once a week. April passed without a hint of top growth. Finally, in late May, as daytime temperatures rose into the 80s and night temperatures remained in the 60s, green pseudostems pushed through the medium and began to unfurl their narrow leaves.

During the years that have passed since that first experiment, I have learned that ginger rhizomes will rot if the potting medium is watered too often during the winter—like the time the pots were placed under a table where water drained onto them from the plants above. I now let the pots of ginger dry out after the leaves begin to turn yellow in early winter.

When the tops are completely brown, the rhizomes are divided and replanted into fresh, moist potting medium and then stored in a dry, shady corner of the greenhouse. These get watered about once a month until March and then the watering is increased to about once a week.

Dormant rhizomes can be potted at any time; however, early spring timing is best for ginger's growing cycle. Propagate new plants by division.

Ginger ready to divide.

Underground, ginger has clusters or "hands" that are rhizomorphous and are referred to as "seeds" by growers. These are thickened, modified underground stems, which produce roots below and shoots above ground. Ginger fingers should be cut with a sterile, sharp knife, at the narrow division between each part of the hand. Leave a few small fingers on the larger seed pieces.

Allow the severed tissue to heal by placing fingers on racks with good air circulation for 24 to 48 hours.

Healing freshly cut rhizomes.

Plant the fingers on top of growing medium, with the growth buds facing up; then cover with the growing medium 1 to 2 inches deep.

In our greenhouse, pots that have sat on the bench, seemingly devoid of life during winter months, send up strong green shoots in late spring, when they are good and ready. In zones 6 and 7, new leaves appear by the end of May.

Ginger "seed" ready to plant.

If forcing the rhizomes to sprout is desired, plant the prepared rhizomes in shallow containers of moistened pasteurized potting medium, clean sand, or coco coir (made from the outer husks of coconuts). Place them on a thermostat-regulated heat mat or other consistently warm surface. Maintain high humidity with mist. Ginger will sprout within 29 days at a constant 78ºF. After the buds sprout, remove the plants from the heat mat and keep them above 50ºF, with strong light, until all danger of frost has passed.

Some years the ginger grows so much that it fills a 5-gallon pot with rhizomes that seem to want to escape out through the drain holes.

Mature ginger saved from frost.

However, in 2022 the yield was small because the ginger was planted directly in garden soil in late June, and we had a drought in Arkansas with triple-digit temperatures for weeks. Planting in early May and providing better irrigation would have produced better results.

Because of the International Herb Association's Herb of the Year™ program, I have been inspired to research designated herbs to improve my cultivation methods. For example, I found out on the Gardening Cook website that commercial ginger rhizomes are sometimes sprayed with a growth inhibitor to keep them from sprouting in cold storage. The remedy for this is to soak the rhizomes in water before planting.

Further research enlightened me to the fact that fresh ginger and turmeric sold in produce markets may be the easiest to obtain but are not the safest propagation stock to use. The danger is that field-grown ginger can carry microscopic nematodes or fungal diseases including bacterial wilt, *Fusarium*, *Pythium*, and *Rhizoctonia*.

To help mitigate this risk, I wondered if hydrogen peroxide might be used as a preventative pretreatment. It took time, but I found a 2018 study, cited in the references, that showed that 2% hydrogen peroxide does suppress the pathogenic fungal organisms on thyme seed and roots that also infect ginger. Given this evidence, though not conclusive, I have decided to spray prewashed ginger seeds with

Diseased ginger rhizomes.

3% hydrogen peroxide and allow the moisture to dry before planting my small crop. Should I ever grow ginger for market, I will purchase tissue-cultured seed ginger to protect garden soil from these diseases.

To grow ginger in soil, according to all the agricultural sites that I researched, during the growing season, farmed ginger needs a soil that is a neutral pH, between 5.5 and 6.5 and, most importantly, well-drained. Incorporating compost or well-rotted barn manure is always recommended. Weed competition must be controlled. The plants require consistent moisture until time for the rhizomes to be harvested. Straw or shredded, aged leaves are recommended for mulch, to retain moisture, suppress annual weeds and to add organic matter.

Though home gardeners are advised to grow ginger in a shady place, a Google keyword search of "ginger farming" produces pictures that portray lush fields of ginger growing in direct sun in Nigeria, Kenya, Uganda, Peru, India, and Hawaii. Ginger grown in full sun produces more rhizomes in comparison to shade-grown ginger, according to studies at North Carolina Agricultural and Technical University. Nonetheless, the leaves do exhibit a sunburned appearance. Home gardeners may prefer more attractive shade-grown plants and not be concerned with higher rhizome yields.

If I were to consider growing commercial ginger, I would use high tunnels to extend the growing season to ten months to optimize the yield and extend the storage life of the crop. Home gardeners must bring potted ginger inside before frost to continue growing. Of course, if fresh ginger is desired from a home-grown plant, a finger may be broken off the side of a rhizome at any time. This baby ginger should be consumed right away. Rhizomes that do not have thick, brown skin do not have a long shelf life.

It is easy to grow your own ginger anywhere you live. All you need is a willingness to experiment, a good rhizome, and understanding of its growth requirements.

References

Abdallah Abdelmegid Mohamed Ali. "Role of hydrogen peroxide in management of root rot and wilt disease of thyme plant." *Journal of Phytopathology and Pest Management*, 5 (3): 1-13, 2018.

"Ginger." Vikispedia. https://vikaspedia.in/agriculture/ crop-production/package-of-practices/spices/ginger. Accessed 2/2/2023.

https://www.researchgate.net/publication/ 337592546_Role_of_hydrogen_peroxide_in_manage- ment_of_root_rot_and_wilt_disease_of_thyme_plant. Accessed 2/4/2023.

Speake, Carol. *The Gardening Cook,* 2/24/21. https://thegar- deningcook.com/growing-ginger/.com. Accessed 2/4/2023.

Snyder, Eli and Lovejoy, Tina. "Ginger and Turmeric: Tropical Superfoods for the Garden." NC Cooperative Extension. Accessed 10/9/2018. https://caldwell.ces.ncsu.edu/2018/10/ginger-and- turmeric-tropical-superfoods-for-the-garden/. Accessed 2/2/ 2023.

Photos by Tina Marie Wilcox.

Tina Marie Wilcox *has been the head gardener and herbalist at the Ozark Folk Center State Park's Heritage Herb Garden, in Mountain View, Arkansas, since 1984. She co-authored the reference book,* <u>the creative herbal home</u>, *with Susan Belsinger. Tina currently serves as president of The International Herb Association, a professional business organization that founded The Herb of the Year™ program.*

GINGERS IN MY FLORIDA GARDEN

Marge Powell

The ginger we herbalists know and love is *Zingiber officinale*, in the family of flowering plants called Zingiberaceae. *Zingiber* is its genus within this family, which contains about 50 different genera with over 1600 known species. *Plants of the World Online*, a database published by Kew Gardens in England, includes 199 plants just of the *Zingiber* genus. Obviously the Zingiberaceae family as a whole is beyond the boundaries of this book, but I write this article to give you a very small and narrow glimpse into the rest of the family through the lens of what grows in my garden here in Northeast Florida (zone 8b/9a). My garden is not unique. The ginger family is a landscape staple in this part of the world.

Edible ginger blooms

Zingiber officinale - Edible Ginger

When I moved to this region 40 years ago, I asked the question, "Which ginger roots are edible?" I was told that any ginger root is edible. I think by "edible" what was meant was, "It won't poison you," because I tried some of the roots of gingers I came across and, while they did not poison me, the taste was too awful to swallow. As a precaution, I went to the grocery store, bought a piece of fresh ginger, and potted it. It grew very well and eventually found its way into my perennial garden; this was the source of my now vigorous plot of ginger. All the gingers in my garden die back in the winter and re-emerge in February.

The leaves of my edible ginger are thinner and more delicate-looking than my other ginger plant leaves and the flower stalk resembles a branch of snapdragon flowers. As these plants started out in the grocery store, I am positive of their source, but not of their species. My research on the internet shows very few illustrations or photos of flowering *Zingiber officinale* that resemble my flowers.

Edible ginger growing in garden.

Hedychium coronarium and *H. flavescens* - White Butterfly & Orange Butterfly or Yellow Ginger Lily

Both plants are beautiful in bloom and their blooms last over a month. They are easy to grow and easily become established in my garden. The scent of the white butterfly ginger is heady, sensual, and lingering. It might be reminiscent of gardenia but there are stronger citrus tones than gardenia. It is a pleasure to work in the garden near these plants when they are in bloom. They are, however, difficult to use as cut flowers, because the many individual flowers emerge from a cone-like structure, one by one. The flowers last a day, then die, and unless you are diligent in picking off the dead flowers, the flowering cone becomes very unattractive.

Zingiber zerumbet - Pinecone or Shampoo Ginger

The pinecone ginger is one of my favorite plants both for its unusual growth habit and its usefulness. The plant is typical of the many gingers that grow here in Florida. In the spring the green foliage appears like the edible ginger. But in the fall short, bracted inflorescences that look like pinecones appear at the base of the plant. These are flower heads which become bright red at maturity. Many people prize these red flower heads for indoor and floral decorations.

The name "shampoo ginger" derives from the practice of squeezing the red cone over the hair as either a shampoo or a conditioner. I have used this as a conditioner, and it works very well but the process has drawbacks. I can only get 2 days' worth of use from a single cone, then the cone will begin to deteriorate. It is also difficult to know exactly how much of the creamy liquid you are using. I have thought of squeezing the liquid into a jar, but I suspect the liquid is better preserved inside the flower cone than by being exposed to light and air. There are many health claims for the rhizome of this plant, from arresting cancers to relieving swollen feet; but I have no experience with the medicinal aspects of this plant, nor do I know of any local herbalist who uses it medicinally.

The pinecone ginger pictured is naturalized in the woods, and there are several fern leaves, which should not be mistaken for the ginger plant leaves.

Kaempheria pulchra – Peacock Ginger

This is a sweet little plant with a growth habit unlike any of the other gingers I grow. It is very low to the ground with a very simple pink flower that only lasts a day. We like it in pots on our patio, but we have friends who grow it as a groundcover in a shady area next to their drive and they find it spreads easily.

Peacock ginger looks very different from the other gingers.

Alpinia zerumbet - Narrow-Leafed Shell Ginger

There are two reasons to grow this ginger. The first is that it loves heavy shade; the second is the showy flower. The flowers are fragrant, and, unlike other gingers, they droop from the end of the stems. The plants can get quite tall, up to six feet here and they are very impressive if there is a massed grouping of them. It is said that in Japan the leaves are used to wrap dumplings and are decocted to a tea. While it is purported to have a role in traditional Eastern medicine, I know of no one using the plant medicinally.

Curcuma longa - Turmeric

Turmeric leaves are much broader than edible ginger leaves.

I also have turmeric growing in my "ginger patch." I have not yet harvested it because I am waiting for the plant to spread more. With all these different ginger plants co-mingling in my perennial garden, I can distinguish them by their leaves. The turmeric leaf is more oblate and has ribs that give a striped effect. Turmeric is also one of the latest plants to emerge in the spring, long after the other gingers. The butterfly ginger leaf is wide with ribbing that forms a "V" pattern. And the edible ginger leaf is narrower and shorter.

Stromanthe sanguinea - Tricolor Ginger

This plant is not in the Zingiberaceae Family, even though it is commonly called tricolor ginger by some. *Stromanthe sanguinea* is a plant species in the arrowroot family Marantaceae native to the Brazilian rainforest. This is the most unusual ginger I grow, for no other reason than I like its coloring. It is a low grower, and it likes shade, so it is growing beneath my large bay tree in my perennial garden. The only practical use I can think of for this plant is that I might, some-day, incorporate the leaves into a floral arrangement. Some-times I just grow things because they are fun.

Alpinia nutans - False Cardamom

This is an interesting plant. It grows in clumps that can get quite large. The leaves are nicely fragrant with a scent that combines cinnamon, citrus, and allspice. The fragrant leaves are one of the best features of this plant. I know of a lo-cal herbalist who uses them for a tea. It is very slow and difficult to bloom. When it blooms, the flowers are like the shell ginger. The flowers die back and leave pods behind, which people can mistake for cardamom, which it is not. True cardamom is *Elet-taria cardamomum*, and the flowers and thus the pods grow from the base of the plant. *Elettaria cardamomum* is too tropical to grow in this area. But we are fortunate to have false cardamom, with its glossy green and fragrant leaves for our shade garden.

References

"Zingiberaceae," *Plants of the World Online.* https://powo.science.kew.org/results?q=Zingiberaceae. Accessed 2-22-23.

Photos by Marge Powell.

Marge Powell has been an herbalist for over 40 years and an avid plant person her entire life. Her herbal interests span culinary, medicinal, body care, as well as growing herbs.

She completed a medicinal herbal apprenticeship with Susun Weed and was introduced to herbal body care in Rosemary Gladstar's workshops. Marge is a passionate cook and most of her cooking is herb-enhanced. She teaches classes in cooking with herbs, and making medicines, lotions, ointments, soaps, and blended fragrances. She has conducted hands-on workshops featuring herbal topics across the United States. In 2011 she created Magnolia Hill Nursery, which wholesales organic herbs and heirloom vegetables to local garden centers.

Marge is currently a board member of the International Herb Association (IHA), the IHA Foundation and is past president of IHA's former Southeastern Region. She has authored numerous herbal articles published in IHA's annual <u>Herb of the Year</u> publications. Recently she has begun collecting data on the history of folk medicine in NE Florida and SE Georgia, hoping to shed some light on this often neglected and unstudied aspect of herbal lore.

Ginger lily, *Hedychium gardnerianum*

This member of the ginger family is a popular ornamental, enjoyed for its beautiful, fragrant blooms. Its anti-cancer medicinal properties are being studied. Best grown in temperate regions, as it can become invasive in tropical climates. Photo taken in California.

Dorene Petersen® 2013

Zingiber officinale, Roscoe.

L. Vietz, 1804. botanicalillustrations.org

THE AMAZING JOURNEY OF GINGER

Kathleen Connole

It is common knowledge that *Zingiber officinale* has been used by humans for some 5,000 years for ceremony, medicine, and food. How did this humble rhizomatous herb become so widespread as to be almost ubiquitous? Ask anyone which spices are on their spice shelf, and we are just about guaranteed that there will be a little jar of ground ginger. The mere thought of this spice causes one to desire the warm, spicy, and sweet flavor of a gingersnap cookie or gingerbread. The natural history of ginger is intertwined with the story of the spice trade, which precedes the first written records of its use.

To trace this species of the family Zingiberaceae to its beginning, one must travel to Southeast Asia. There is debate as to whether it was first cultivated in southern China or India, or both. There are wild relatives still to be found growing in India.

We are familiar with the stories of the spice trade and the Silk Road. Caravans of traders on camels, specially bred for being able to walk on sand, traveled over 4,000 miles, from the second century BCE until the mid-1400s, to bring silk textiles, exotic spices and incense, tea, and porcelain from the Far East to be traded with Egypt, Greece, and Rome. The journey was long and dangerous, crossing deserts and the highest mountain ranges in the world, with constant threats from nomadic raiders and bandits. The entire trip would take a year and the goods exchanged hands several times along the way to middlemen at trading posts, who made the greatest profit. The term "Silk Road" was coined by German geographer and traveler Ferdinand von Richthofen in the late 1800s, and while the fine Chinese silk was originally most desired by the Roman elite class, in later years it was the spices—pepper, cloves, nutmeg, and ginger—that were the main items of trade. Whoever controlled this trade could attain great wealth. (nationalgeographic.org).

The role of spices in the history of world trade and the eventual globalization that exists today cannot be underestimated. Some of the other items exchanged also had huge impacts, including paper and gunpowder from China to the West, as well as horses and the art of glassmaking from the West to China.

The entire scope of the spice trade is better described as "Silk (or "Spice") Routes." There was a "large network of strategically located trading posts, markets, and thoroughfares, designed to streamline the transport, exchange, distribution, and storage, of goods" (history.com). The land route stretched from the ancient Greco-Roman metropolis and across the Syrian desert through Iraq, across the mountains and through Iran, Turkmenistan, and Afghanistan to Mongolia and China. There were ports on the Persian Gulf where goods could be carried on boats up the Tigris and Euphrates Rivers.

Long before the overland trade routes from China to the Red Sea, there was what is called by some the "maritime silk road." The people of the archipelagos of the Pacific, the area later known as the East Indies, had been trading their "forest products" (including ginger) with the Chinese and the peoples of ancient India, since the second century BCE.

Some 6,000 years ago, humans now known as Austronesians began to migrate from southern China. By 3,300 years ago they had spread from island to island in the archipelagos now known as Indonesia, the Philippines, Malaysia, and Oceania (Polynesia, Micronesia, and Melanesia), traveling hundreds of miles at a time. The name "Austronesian" refers to a language family of related peoples who are first believed to have come from Taiwan. The word comes from "austral" meaning southern, and "nesia", islands. Successive generations, many of whom we now know as Polynesians, spread some 6,500 miles throughout the Indo-Pacific oceans, and today some 270 million people speak languages with their roots in ancient Austronesian.

There are over 1,200 closely related islands, including modern-day well-known Sumatra, Java, Borneo, Malaysia, Timor, New Guinea, the Mariannas, the Philippines, New Zealand, and Easter Island. The island of Madagascar, across the Indian Ocean, off the east coast of Africa, was eventually settled as well. Descendants of the Austronesians first reached the Hawaiian Islands around 940 to 1,130 AD.

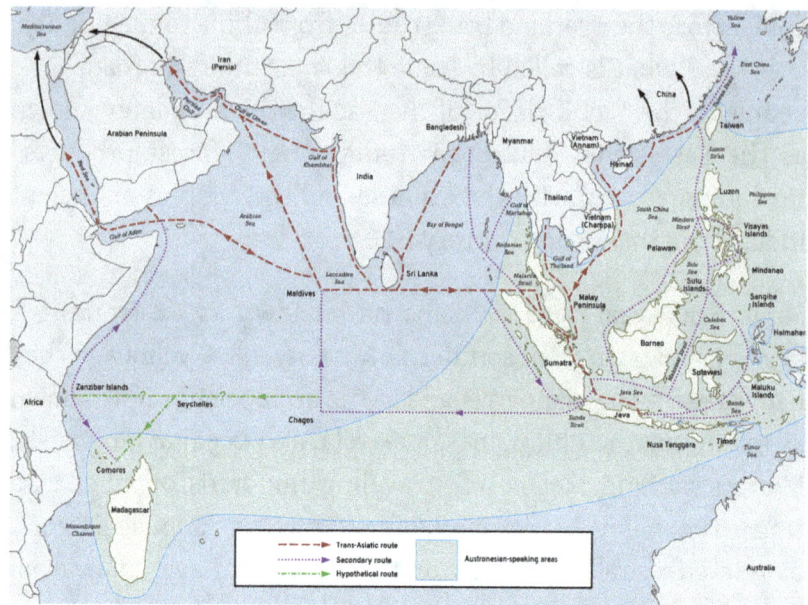

Austronesian maritime trade routes, 1200 CE.
creativecommons.org

Also included are the Moluccas, or "Spice Islands," a tiny group of islands located at the intersection of Asia and Oceania, on the equator, north of Australia and west of New Guinea. They were the only place in the world where cloves (*Syzygium aromaticum*) and nutmeg (*Myristica fragrans*) were endemic. The spices of the Moluccas were the most coveted and valuable of any trade item.

Nutmeg trees could only be found in the ten tiny volcanic Banda islands, found in the Banda Sea, 1,243 miles east of Java. These islands had been inhabited for thousands of years. The trees that produced cloves grew only on the islands of Ternate and Tidore. The natives of these islands were part of the ancient Austronesian maritime trade network, and traded with India and Arabia long before the Europeans discovered their location.

The Austronesian people were the world's first mariners. The earliest known group, known as the Lapita, developed sailing technologies at least 3,500 years ago specific to their needs. The voyaging canoes were large enough to hold families, their provisions, and a cargo of plants and animals, seaworthy enough to travel long distances and survive all weather conditions encountered. The Polynesians later refined the boats with wave splitters and splash boards and embellished them with carvings of symbolic cultural images.

The Austronesians displayed remarkable ingenuity in their boat-building and navigational skills. The outrigger boats were constructed from native trees and plant fibers, using stone tools. These vessels made possible the settlement of the multitude of islands of the South Pacific and the maritime trade route across the Indian Ocean to India and the east coast of Africa. The large trading outrigger canoes were still in use in the late 1800s and written about by Ernest Way Elkington in his book *The Savage South Seas*: "... it consists of three canoes lashed together and boarded over. On these boards is a kind of a barn cut down and spread out considerably. This is used both for shelter and for carrying the pots and articles of barter. From the centre of this raft-like barge the two enormous sails project straight into the air; the two horn-like points of the top are decorated with long streamers ... [These boats are] used for long trips, and carry big crews, being often loaded to their full carrying capacity" (57).

Indonesian outrigger trading canoe,
W.H. Handy, 1872.
projectgutenberg.org

The people are the spirit of the canoe;
the canoe is the spirit of the people.
---Maori saying
(Indigenous people of New Zealand)

By 1778, when Captain Cook was on his third voyage across the Pacific, the Austronesians inhabited islands stretching from New Zealand in the south, to Hawaii and Easter Island in the east, to Madagascar in the west. According to Brian Lavery in *The Conquest of the Ocean*, Cook marveled that they had accomplished this in simple boats without the aid of charts or compasses. Joseph Banks, Cook's naturalist, observed that the boats "are frequently upset but the people are almost amphibious and care little for such accidents ... [They were] such good swimmers that only seals can be compared with them" (p. 14).

In the PBS Nova article "Polynesia's Genuis Navigators" presenter Liesl Clark observed: "They approached the open ocean with great respect; no other culture embraced the open sea so fully ... The paths of the stars and the rhythms of the ocean guided them by night, and the color of the sky and the sun, the shapes of the clouds, and the direction from which the swells were coming, guided them by day" (pbs.org).

The predictable, seasonal winds of the monsoons, an intimate knowledge of the ocean's currents, and the tropical climate, in which the sun and stars were most often visible, were taken advantage of by these earliest mariners.

The Pacific Ocean is the largest geographical feature on earth, covering nearly one-third of its surface. Most of the islands being discussed here have equatorial tropical climates, except for Hawaii (which is tropical, although north of the equator); New Zealand and Easter Island are temperate and subtropical. The geology of the islands changes from west to east. The western islands are formed from continental-type rocks and are thought to be part of the ancient super-continent Gondwanaland, that split apart 167 million years ago. Over most of the Pacific basin the islands are *oceanic*, meaning that they are composed of ancient volcanic basalt rock, and range in age from very recent to almost 20 million years old. The *high islands* are volcanic domes; the highest is Hawaii with two peaks over 13,000 feet.

Over millions of years other islands have eroded to at or below sea level; *low islands* that over time have become surrounded by coral reefs are known as *atolls*. They are covered by a limestone cap up to hundreds of meters thick, above the original basalt base. The geology affects the types of plant life to be found naturally on these islands. The atolls are of "superb beauty ... [with] azure and turquoise-blue central lagoons with chains of coral and sand islets ... strung out like pearls of a necklace along all or part of the perimeter ... in stark contrast to harsh living conditions that allow only a limited number of terrestrial plant species" (Whistler 2-3).

The Austronesians wisely carried with them ginger and other "canoe plants," plants so important to them for food, fiber, medicine, and ritual, that they fit them into their outrigger canoes along with their entire families and necessities. They settled along the coastal areas where they found favorable conditions. Survival at the beginning would depend solely upon food from the sea and whatever few native plants grew there, for months or even years, until the propagules that they brought with them became established.

According to Lynton Dove White, "Upon the sailing canoes were stashed precious cargo of the shoots, roots, cuttings, and seeds of these plants for food, cordage, medicine, fabric, containers; all of life's vital needs ... This was a culture without clay or iron whose people knew the intrinsic value of the cargo they carried beyond the horizon."

The importance of the rhizome of *Z. officinale* in medicinal and religious practices to the ancient people, more so than as a food, ensured that it was one of the essential plants to be carried in the canoes. Ginger was believed to provide protection and bring good fortune to these people of the sea.

Besides ginger, some of the plants that they transported and planted wherever they landed included: Candlenut, taro, breadfruit, jackfruit, yams, sweet potatoes (*Ipomoea batatas*), bamboo, gourds, coconut, Job's tears, citrus, *Ficus* species, banana, rice, *Piper* species, sugar cane, arrowroot, and the Zingiberaceae family, including galangal (*Alpinia galanga*), ginger (*Z. officinale*), and shampoo ginger (*Z. zerumbet*). Many of these plants have in common the fact that they are propagated from rhizomes and provided staple carbohydrate-containing foods. Others could be propagated by seed. Both forms could be carried for long distances and remain viable.

The fact that sweet potatoes were an important food crop for these people since ancient times strongly suggests that they were able to cross the Pacific and obtain them from their native land of the Andes mountains of South America. The latest scientific genetic studies have confirmed that there was contact between the people of Easter Island and South America 19 to 23 generations ago, between 1300 and 1500 AD (smithsonianmag.com).

The sweet potato is the food that ends famine quickly.

--- Kanaka Maoli, the Indigenous people of Hawaii

The Austronesians and their descendants were gatherers and gardeners rather than agriculturists. To succeed at cultivating their chosen plants, they had to possess horticultural knowledge of each one's growing requirements, how to keep them alive as they traveled, and how to propagate them. They took advantage of the climate and growing conditions in the islands where they settled. They had no beasts of burden. In addition to the plants listed, they cultivated fruit and nut trees, and they knew how to grow rice and millet since coming from Taiwan.

There is little archeological evidence of plant use due to the tropical climate that ensures rapid decomposition. Remnants of tools used in gardening and food processing have been found and provide clues about the plants that they used. However, descendants of these people have continued to grow and use the same plants; the knowledge of their uses has been passed down through the generations. The strongest evidence is the proliferation and naturalization of these plants throughout the areas that were settled by the Austronesians.

In addition to food plants, canoe plants were important sources of materials for medicine, ritual, plaiting, cordage, clothing, housing, canoe-building, fishing, crafts, ornamentation, musical instruments, and toys.

Ginger is now known to be one of the earliest plants to be cultivated and *Z. officinale* has long depended upon humans for propagation, as it rarely blooms or produces viable seeds.

Shampoo ginger (*Zingiber zerumbet*) was also widely used; it no longer grows wild, but survives in naturalized populations to this day in Hawaii. Of the 50 to 60 known canoe plants, it is now known that only about 26 made it as far as Hawaii.

Other plants related to ginger but less commonly used included *Curcuma longa*, turmeric; *Etlingera elatior*, torch ginger; *Alpinia nutans*, dwarf cardamom; *Amomum acre*, panasa cardamom; *Curcuma zedoaria*, white turmeric; and *Hedychium coronarium*. white ginger lily.

In Hawaii, the liquid produced by flowers of Z. zerumbet
was used for shampoo and hair
conditioner; this was also used
to quench thirst. The leaves
and leaf stalks were used
in underground ovens to enhance the flavor of pork and
fish. The rhizome, dried and
powdered, was used for the
fragrance it imparted to tapa
cloth. Medicinally it was used
throughout Polynesia for digestive upsets, skin infections,
cuts, sprains, toothaches, and
headaches (White).

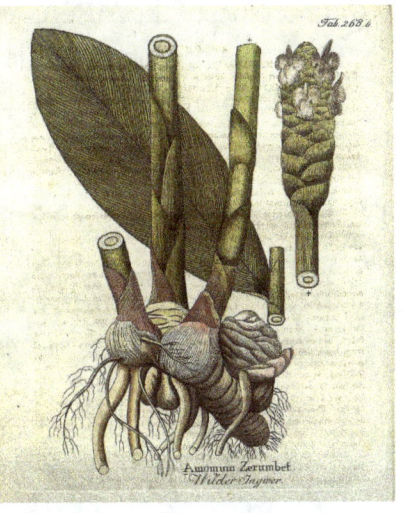

**Shampoo ginger was a familiar garden
plant in Europe by the 19th century.**
*Zingiber zerumbet (L.) Roscoe ex Sm., Vietz, F.B.,
1806. plantillustrations.org*

Since ginger rhizomes freshly
dug are very perishable, in the earliest times they would be
dried in the sun to preserve them for the long journey ahead.
When sugar cane, another canoe plant, became widely available,
methods of preservation using sugar were developed.

> In the earliest history of the spice trade, cloves, nutmeg,
> and ginger were transported by the Austronesians via
> the seas to India, where black pepper (*Piper nigrum*) grew.
> *Zingiber officinale* became widely cultivated in Sri Lanka.
> The Latin genus name *Zingiber, zingiberi,* is from Pali, the
> classical language of southern Buddhism, as *singivera,*
> "horned root."

By the time of the Greek physician Dioscorides, ginger was also
being grown by the Indians on the eastern coast of Africa, 5,000

miles from its origins. Some of his earliest written words show its importance: "they use it fresh, boiling it for soups and ... stews ... some producers pickle it ... Its effect is warming, digestive, gently laxative, appetizing; it helps in cases of cataract, and it is an ingredient in antidotes against poison" (Dalby, 156).

The Indian traders as middlemen transported spices including ginger to the Red Sea, where the Arabs in turn traded with the Greeks and Romans of the Mediterranean: "... [Early] Arab traders protected their passages and personal supplies of ginger from the inquisitive and resourceful Greeks and Romans by actually fabricating a fabled land inhabited by a primitive and ruthless people they called the Troglodytes" (Schulick, 8).

The Roman Empire extended throughout Europe, where the wealthy classes became enamored with the exotic flavors. Roman cuisine was "laden with spices, especially white pepper, cloves, grains of paradise, and ginger" (Dalby 132).

After the fall of the Roman Empire, the Arabs had complete control of the spice trade. The costs increased so much that only the very wealthy could afford them. "Spices were ... regarded as antidotes to earthly squalor in another, more mystical sense [and were] thought to be hauled from the Nile in nets, having washed down the river from Paradise ... where exotic plants grew in abundance" (Standage 67).

As Jack Turner states in his book *Spice, the History of a Temptation*, in the chapter titled "The Spice of Love", "... medieval Europe's appetite for exotic Eastern spices was fueled by an unholy matrimony of lust and gluttony" (p. 187). The early fourteenth century kitchen pantry of the widow of King Charles IV of France, Jeanne d'Evreux, held 6 pounds of pepper, 13 1/2 pounds of cinnamon, 5 pounds of grains of paradise, a small quantity of mace, and "a colossal 23 1/2 pounds of ginger ... the widow's stockpile was impressive but by no means exceptional" (Turner 106).

Spices including ginger had been combined with incense as part of religious rituals since ancient times. They also became a part of the cuisine of monks, although only the servants were allowed to add them to the food. During the season of Lent, when meat was not allowed, spices were consumed in large amounts to flavor the fish, liqueurs, and wines. "... [T]he monks had no qualms about quaffing pepper, ginger, cumin, sage, and a thousand such types of seasonings, which delight the palate but inflame the libido ... it was a foolhardy monk who nourished his body but hazarded the security of his soul on such dangerous foods ... salt and hunger were the only acceptable seasonings for his cabbage, bread, beans, and lentils" (Turner 273).

Ginger had been widely grown in China and India for many years prior to the arrival of the first European explorers. Marco Polo, Magellan, and Da Gama all returned with observations of ginger plantations and the wealth that they brought to those that controlled the supply. Once the true source of the spices was revealed, the Age of Exploration began in the 1400s, with European powers competing to find routes to the Spice Islands and gain control of the spice trade.

"... from a European perspective ... the mystery of and the appeal of spices [prompted] them to uncover the true origins of these strangely appealing dried roots, shriveled berries, desiccated twigs, slivers of bark, and sticky bits of gum—with momentous consequences in the course of human history" (Standage 68).

The Italians, Spanish, Portuguese, Dutch, and English in turn gained control with devastating effects on the indigenous peoples of the spice-growing regions. By the 1500s, Spain had established the now well-known Jamaican ginger plantations. As the colonial powers were able to grow spices in their tropical colonies, they became more commonplace and thus less expensive and desirable. Other items of trade were more profitable, such as tea, rubber, tobacco, and coffee. The chile peppers of the Americas were less expensive than black pepper and could be grown in the temperate climates.

Tastes changed in Europe as well, as the cultures changed. The Puritan and later the Victorian ethics would not favor such spices as ginger with a reputation as an aphrodisiac. Simpler, fresher flavors were favored in cuisines. Sugar became plentiful and affordable, and the use of ginger was limited to sweet desserts.

There are many stories about gingerbread and its popularity in Europe. The most ostentatious display of this infatuation occurred "around the year 1400, when the Parisian merchant Jacques Duché had a walk-in gingerbread house constructed, its walls inlaid with precious stones and spices" (Turner 131).

When Europeans settled in America, they took with them their recipes using ginger. In *American Household Botany*, Judith Sumner states that the Shakers at Mount Lebanon, New York, grew ginger as a medicinal plant and used it for tonics, stomach ailments, and cholera. They obtained the rhizomes from Jamaica, and treated them as annuals, saving the rhizomes over winter to be replanted in the growing season. They also cultivated wild ginger, *Asarum canadense*, and used it similarly.

Sumner also tells us that George Washington served ginger cakes and rum punch to prospective voters. In 1824, Mary Randolph described two types of "ginger bread"—one was "plebian" and made with "pearl ash"; the other was a richer "sugar ginger bread" which was leavened with a dozen eggs and "a large cupful of powdered ginger and brandy" (191).

In 1844 Sumner says that there were two basic gingerbreads: a cakelike variety made with molasses, and a "hard ginger-bread" made with caraway and rolled out on pans for baking. Some cooks preserved ginger rhizomes in syrup for later use as a sweetmeat, and to be passed around after meals to promote digestion. Ginger beer and wine and medicinal ginger teas are also mentioned in Sumner's book.

It is interesting to note that as Western tastes became blander and ginger was relegated to sweets, the cuisines of the East became known for being spicy and hot; they easily incorporated the capsicums that were original to America. It does make sense that dishes using fresh ginger, such as pickled ginger and stir-fry, would be more popular in the lands where it originated and can grow naturally.

It is no surprise that members of the ginger family were grown as ornamentals in British gardens of the 1800s, particularly by the Victorians, since many of them have lovely, unusual, and fragrant blooms.

In botanical nomenclature we will often see ginger listed with a name that aroused my curiosity; *Zinger officinale* (L.) Roscoe. Who was this "Roscoe"? William Roscoe (1753-1831) was an English historian, banker, lawyer, art collector, botanist, aboli-tionist, poet, and Member of Parliament. His father was a market gardener and tavern keeper. Young William left school at the age of 12 and worked in his father's garden, using his free time reading and studying.

William corresponded with Thomas Jefferson, was admired by Washington Irving, and one of his poems was set to music by George III for the king's daughter.

When Roscoe retired, he set to work publishing a monograph on the reorganization of the plant family Zingiberaceae. The work included drawings, "Chiefly Drawn from Living Specimens in the Botanical Gardens in Liverpool." William Roscoe's daughter-in-law, Margaret, was an accomplished botanical artist and her work is included in her father's work and in *Floral Illustrations of the Seasons* published in 1829.

If I were asked now whom I consider to be

the happiest of the human race,

I should answer,

those who cultivate the earth by their own hands.

---William Roscoe

Finally, ginger and its close relatives are still known as beautiful plants in the garden, and even if one does not live in a tropical climate, they can be planted in spring and enjoyed throughout the growing season; they are easily kept in pots and protected over the winter, to be replanted in spring. And, if we include the edible and medicinal *Zingiber officinale*, we can harvest some of its rhizome to be enjoyed and benefited from in a multitude of ways.

References

Abbott, Isabella Alona. *Traditional Uses of Hawaiian Plants.* Bishop Museum Press, 1992.

"Canoes and Their Construction: Navigating the Sea of Islands." https://archives.anu.edu.au/exhibitions/navigating-sea-islands/canoes-and-their-construction. Accessed 2/5/23.

Clark, Leisl. "Ancient Worlds – Polynesia's Genius Navigators." *Nova Newsletter.* https://www.pbs.org/wgbh/nova/article/polynesia-genius-navigators/. Accessed 2/19/23.

Dalby, Andrew. *Dangerous Tastes: The Story of Spices.* University of California Press, 2000.

"Domesticated plants and animals of Austronesia." (268 references cited.) https://www.wikipedia.org/wiki/Domesticated_plants_and_animals_of_Austronesia. Accessed 10/10//22.

Elkington, Ernest W. *The Savage South Seas.* A&C Black, 1907. https://www.gutenberg.org/files/57695/57695-h/57695-h.htm. Accessed 2/19/23.

Fulder, Stephen. *The Ginger Book: The Ultimate Home Remedy.* Avery Publishing Group, 1996.

Hamilton, Roy W. "The Legacy of Indo-Pacific Voyaging." https://fowler.ucla.edu/a-look-back-at-the-art-of -austronesians-the-legacy-of-indo-pacific-voyaging/ Accessed 2/5/23.

Handwerk, Brian. "The Polynesians." *Smithsonian Science.* https://www.smithsonianmagazine.com/science-nature/native-americans-polynesians-meet-1809752691. Accessed 2/19/23.

Krondl, Michael. *The Taste of Conquest: The Rise and Fall of the Three Great Cities of Spice.* Ballantine Books, 2007.

Lavery, Brian. *The Conquest of the Ocean.* DK Publishing, 2013.

Laws, Bill. *Fifty Plants that Changed the Course of History.* Quid Publishing, 2010.

"Maritime Silk Road." https://www.en.wikipedia.org/wiki/Maritime_Silk_Road. Accessed 2/4/23.

"Maluka Islands." https://www.en.wikipedia.org/wiki/Maluka_Islands. Accessed 10/13/22.

"Roscoe, William." Encyclopedia Brittanica. https://en.wikipedia.org/wiki/Encyclopaedia_Britannica_William_Roscoe. Accessed 2/19/23.

Riley, Carroll, ed. *Man Across the Sea: Problems of Pre-Columbian Contacts.* University of Texas Press, 1971.

Schulick, Paul. *Ginger: Common Spice and Wonder Drug.* 3 ed, Hohm Press,1996.

"Silk Road.." *National Geographic.* www.nationalgeographic.org/resource/silk-road. Accessed 2/6/23.

"Silk Routes." https://www.history.com/topics/ancient-middle-east/silk-road. Accessed 2/6/23.

Smith, Bruce D. *The Emergence of Agriculture.* Scientific American Library, 1995.

"Spice Islands (Moluccas): 250 Years of Maps (1521-1760)." https://www.lib_dbserver.princeton.edu/visual_materials/maps/websites/pacific/spice-islands-maps.html. Accessed 11/15/22.

Sumner, Judith. *American Household Botany: A History of Useful Plants 1620-1900.* Timber Press, 2004.

Standage, Tom. *An Edible History of Humanity.* Walker & Company, 2009.

Turner, Jack. Spice: *The History of a Temptation.* Alfred A. Knopf, 2004.

White, Lynton Dove. *Canoe Plants of Ancient Hawaii.* https://canoeplants.com. Accessed 2/22/23.

Whistler, W. Arthur. *Plants of the Canoe People: An Ethnobotanical Voyage Through Polynesia.* National Tropical Botanical Garden, 2009.

Kathleen Connole *joined the Ozark Folk Center's Heritage Herb Garden team in 2006. Before moving to Arkansas' Buffalo River Country in 2005, Kathleen earned a degree in Plant Science from the University of Missouri-Columbia and worked at Powell Gardens and Farrand Farms in Kansas City, Missouri.*

Kathleen researches the natural history of the Heritage Herb Garden's diverse herbal collection. She composes interpretive signage for the Garden to tell the stories of these plants.

Kathleen served as chair and is an active member of the Herb Society of America Ozark Unit, headquartered at the Ozark Folk Center State Park. She currently is secretary for the International Herb Association Board. She was editor of the IHA's Viola, Herb of the Year™ 2022, *and is now the editor of* Ginger, Herb of the Year™ 2023.

*In the nearby Dobu Islands, shamans chewed and spat ginger
at the "seat" of an illness to cure it, while at sea sailors
did the same to halt oncoming storms.*

---"Dobu Medicine." *encyclopedia.com*

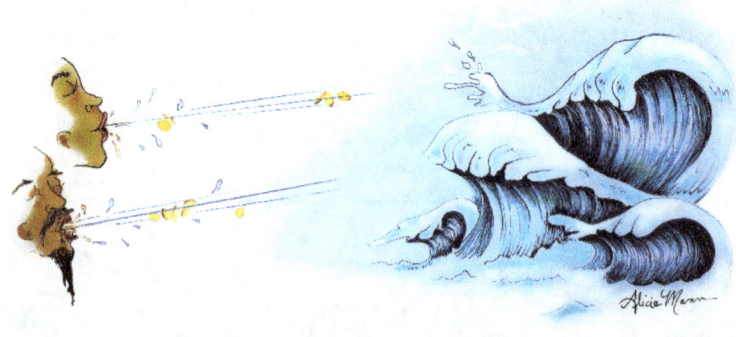

Spitting Ginger to Calm the Tempest.
Alicia Mann

THE SPIT AND IMAGE OF GINGER

Gert Coleman

An ancient Asian proverb, "Every good quality is contained in ginger," speaks to ginger's curative, culinary, and magical powers across the ages. In fact, around the world the use of ginger (*Zingiber officinale*) has been interwoven into the rhythms of daily life, from rituals for prosperity and protection to colorful usage in language and literature. And its pungent scent and spicy flavor have led many cultures to treat it as a gift from the gods, attributing supernatural powers to this golden root.

Warm and spicy to the tongue, yet soothing to the digestive system, ginger blends well with many spices and enhances a variety of cuisines. Adding ginger to your life can promote circulation, alleviate nausea, ease coughs, reduce inflammation, enliven your cooking, and spice up your sex life. Over fifty percent of Asian medicinal remedies include ginger. When in doubt, start with ginger.

Eastern Beliefs and Practices

The use of ginger originated in Asia, where it grew wild and abundantly. Asian Indians believed ginger could bring you closer to the gods. Before religious ceremonies, they avoided eating strong-smelling garlic and onion for fear of offensive odors "but they ate lots of ginger because it left them smelling sweet and therefore presentable to the gods" (Castleman 186).

In one welcoming African ritual, a shaman would chew ginger then spit it forcefully into guests' faces, wetting the cheeks.

Before sea voyages, Austronesians rubbed ship hulls and sails with fresh ginger to ward off evil and safeguard the crew. For long sea voyages in the 1300s, Chinese traders traveled with their families in small cabins on their boats, using wooden tubs to grow ginger and other herbs for cooking and medicine (Fulder 83). Chinese sailors chewed ginger to prevent seasickness and Chinese women drank ginger tea for morning sickness, menstrual cramps, and other gynecological problems. Considered an antidote to shellfish poisoning, ginger is an essential seasoning in many Asian fish recipes (Castleman 187).

In the Trobriand Islands, an archipelago off the coast of New Guinea, shamans chewed and spat ginger to bless crops and keep their settlements safe. In a complicated ritual to prevent or cure illness, a shaman would place ginger in a conch shell while praying, then close the shell with a banana leaf to keep the prayers within. The shell was then placed into a conical bag with a wild ginger leaf and another banana leaf. At the appointed time, shamans blew out the conch shells at the northern and southern borders of the village. For further protection and intimidation, fresh ginger root would be chewed and discharged at intruders (*EccentricNature*).

In the nearby Dobu Islands, shamans chewed and spat ginger at the "seat" of an illness to cure it, while at sea sailors did the same to halt oncoming storms (*Enc* 112). Tribes in Papua-New Guinea chewed ginger to heat up the body before religious rituals while sailors expelled chewed ginger into laden canoes to protect cargo from disasters at sea. On land, shamans expectorated ginger onto village entrance roads to ward off misfortune and hunger and to bring good fortune (Fulder 81).

Today, ginger is still widely revered throughout Asia for food, medicine, and hope for the future. In Hong Kong temples, participants hang ginger in large paper constructions as offerings to promote fertility and prosperity (Fulder 84). In addition, Asians often grow ginger outside the front door to invite plenitude and protection into their lives. In colder climes, you can easily grow ginger as a houseplant near the entrance to invite wealth and riches into your life.

Western Magic, Myth and Folklore

Through the spice trade, ginger arrived in the Mediterranean and spread through Europe, where it has been highly regarded as a catalyst for strengthening spells as well as immune systems.

Astrologically, ginger falls under the planet Mars, associated with the element of Fire, thus utilized to speed rituals along. According to magical herbalist Scott Cunningham, ginger's heat ensures efficacy in the areas of Money, Success, Power and Prosperity (*Enc* 112). Thus, in various forms, ginger is added to smudge sticks, incense, sachets, and amulets; used to anoint candles; cooked or infused with other magical herbs; and burned to consecrate tools. Ginger can be chewed with cinnamon to enhance rituals for both financial and courtship success.

Ginger's fiery heat, associated with passion, is a natural for Love spells. As far back as *The Arabian Nights*, ginger has been favored as an aphrodisiac. Heating the blood and improving circulation equals feeling sexy or "hot blooded". The longer you cook ginger, the hotter it tastes. Thus, ginger has long been the go-to spice to "heat things up" in either a new relationship or to reinvigorate one that has grown cold.

Remember the song "Love Potion # 9"? Ginger may have been part of that formula. According to Cunningham, love spells and potions, performed with good intent, are best used to "place you in situations where you will meet people, overcome shyness, and communicate that you are in the mood for love" (*Enc* 17-18). Powdered ginger combines well with lemon balm, cardamom, cinnamon, and vanilla for a fragrant love incense. Dried ginger chips can accent roses and cinnamon sticks for an alluring pot-pourri. To make a simple love charm, tuck ginger chips into a small muslin bag to carry in your pocket or purse. Or steep citrusy ginger slices in wine to create a love libation.

Noted as Masculine in gender—just look at that root! —ginger's essential oil is considered magnetic, especially to attract men. Mars is associated with Tuesday, a good day to perform spells and rituals to promote passion and bravery. Associated colors include scarlet, red, orange, and black, symbolic of flames, to be added as ribbons, candles, or amulet bags. The zodiac sign Aries (March 21 to April 19) is ruled by Mars; associated plants include lots of warming herbs like allspice, chiles, garlic, pepper, and, of course, ginger (*Garden Witch's Herbal* 222).

To acquire divine masculine energy, particularly in warrior situations, bathe in a ginger bath or anoint yourself with diluted ginger oil. Ellen Dugan suggests combining ginger oil with basil oil, black pepper oil, a holly leaf, and a small jasper chip to be stored in a red glass bottle, tied with a red or black ribbon to tap into the Martian hues of power (*Book of Witchery* 94-95).

Ginger can attract fish as well. According to British fishing folklore, "when ginger is chewed and the juice is applied to the bait, the fish really flock to the hook" (Hayes 40).

And if you suffer from nightmares, either put a whole ginger root under the bed or tuck a few ginger chips into a sleep pillow to get a good night's sleep.

Ginger in Literature

Fairytales, historical fiction, and poetry can bring an herb or spice to life, offering background knowledge for readers to remember and use. In addition, plant descriptions depict setting and act as images to add depth to plot, character, and mood. Ginger quite naturally adds a spicy pungency to Literature.

Though many consider fairytales to be children's stories, they can also reveal the real-life horrors faced by medieval folk trying to survive in challenging times. For example, ensnared in the deprivations of the 14th century, two starving children, Hansel and Gretel, contend with parental estrangement, enslavement, attempted cannibalism, and even murder. This tale reverses the warm, positive images of ginger when an evil witch uses a gingerbread house to attract the children inside.

Abandoned during a prolonged famine, Hansel and Gretel are lost in the forest when they come across that famous gingerbread house. Hansel eats part of the roof while Gretel nibbles on the wall. Once inside, the witch captures them, fattening Hansel up for the kill. Through luck, ingenuity, and faith in God, the children survive and escape.

Hansel and Gretel illustration, 1909.
Arthur Rackham, Public Domain

"Hansel and Gretel" accurately depicts a historical period "of great dearth" (Lang 251) spanning the 13th through 17th centuries, when the Little Ice Age shortened growing seasons and exacerbated winters, leaving millions dead of starvation and disease in Central and Eastern Europe. "Shortage of wheat for bread—the staple diet of the common people—led to frequent bread riots. Shortage of fodder meant fewer animals could be overwintered, resulting in a decline of flocks and herds, and so a decrease in the food supply" (Swinfen 271). Starvation was so pervasive that the illusion of a gingerbread house was exceptionally alluring.

By the time the Grimm Brothers collected and published the tale in the early 1800s, "Hansel and Gretel" was over 400 years old. Though the image of the sparkling gingerbread house is what often comes to mind when we think of this story, ironically there is no actual gingerbread in the original description: "... the cottage was made of bread and roofed with cakes, while the window was made of transparent sugar" (Lang 254). It is a testament to the popularity and love of gingerbread that it has become so closely associated with this tale.

During his reign (1509-1547), King Henry VIII encouraged the use of ginger as a plague preventative and his daughter Elizabeth I (1558-1603) consumed a powdered ginger concoction to settle her stomach. Under their rule, eating gingerbread at court flourished—no doubt contributing to Henry's obesity—and soon became a national phenomenon. In fact, according to food writer Sarah Nicolls, "In the 1600s, in a number of European countries gingerbread baking was considered a profession of its own. Apparently only professional gingerbread bakers had permission to bake gingerbread, apart from at Christmas and Easter when anybody was allowed to do so, such was its importance!"

Town fairs, the local centers of English commerce, attracted vendors and consumers, with competing gingerbread bakers offering a variety of shapes and characters—babies, adults, and animals. Gingerbread men were called "husbands" and were often shaped with exaggerated phalluses, eliciting much ribaldry (Fulder 81). In a more scholastic vein, Dutch children in the 17th century used gingerbread letters to learn their alphabet. By the 1800s, gingerbread houses were a long-standing tradition in much of Europe and the British Isles, particularly during the Christmas holidays, and "Hansel and Gretel" popularized gingerbread houses even further.

Ginger's healthful aspects appear in *The Long Winter*, an American novel of survival and ingenuity by Laura Ingalls Wilder. As new settlers on the harsh Dakota prairie, the Ingalls try to prepare for an unexpectedly hard winter. Charles Ingalls grew several acres of hay but had no help to harvest it. While Ma is not happy about her daughters doing men's work, Laura gamely helps Pa gather the hay. It is hot, dry, exhausting work:

Now the sun and the wind were hotter and Laura's legs quivered while she made them trample the hay. She was glad to rest for the little times between the field and the stack. She was thirsty, then she was thirstier, and then she was so thirsty that she could think of nothing else. It seemed forever till ten o'clock when Carrie came lugging the jug half-full.

Pa told Laura to drink first but not too much. Nothing was ever so good as that cool wetness going down her throat. At the taste of it she stopped in surprise and Carrie clapped her hands and cried out, laughing, "Don't tell, Laura, don't tell till Pa tastes it!"

Ma had sent them ginger-water. She had sweetened the cool well-water with sugar, flavored it with vinegar, and put in plenty of ginger to warm their stomachs so they could drink till they were not thirsty. Ginger-water would not make them sick, as plain cold water would when they were so hot.

Such a treat made that ordinary day into a special day, the first day that Laura helped in the haying.

According to food writer Melissa Norris, "What Ma made was sweet ginger water to help quench thirst, cool the body, and replenish the calcium and magnesium lost from a hard day's labor ... when you are hot and on the brink of dehydration, plain water may not be the best for you. For some, it can make their stomach very upset, causing nausea, cramping and other uncomfortable problems."

The Semantics of Ginger

Linguistically, the term *ginger* has both positive and negative connotations, and is often considered insulting. Nicknames include *carrot top*, *ginger nut*, *Duracell* (the "coppertop" battery), and *gingivitis*. Ironically, *gingivitis* (gum disease) and *gingerly* (hesitantly) derive from different word roots and have nothing to do with this spicy root.

The image of ginger often conjures the colors red and orange, especially a red-haired individual, called a *ginger*, defined by *Urban Dictionary* as "One who has coloured hair ranging in shades from Red to Strawberry blonde. Usually pale with freckles ... more susceptible to sunlight." Why are redheads called gingers? One theory likens the ginger color to the reddish-brown tinge of gingerbread and ginger cookies. Another theory suggests that ginger's fiery taste symbolizes the hot tempers associated with redheads. Some ginger root varieties, particularly in Malaysia, have red flowers and reddish roots. And ginger sometimes turns reddish when pickled.

Stereotypically, red hair has been associated with being hot-headed, and for millennia redheads have been bullied, shunned, mistreated, and targeted. The Ancient Greeks believed redheads were vampiric by nature, and religious art typically depicts Mary Magdalene and Judas Iscariot as having red hair. Some believed redheads to be descended from Prometheus, the mythical bringer of fire, and that the first Ginger was the flame he brought to the human race. Thus, the belief persisted that "all

Gingers have had the fire of Prometheus coursing through their veins, scorching their hair bright red, charring their skin into what are commonly mistaken for freckles when the fire strays too close to the surface." This ancient prejudice towards red-heads is called *gingerism* and the fear of them is *gingerphobia* (*Urbandictionary.com*).

Conversely, the Greeks also associated red hair with love, beauty, and sexual passion. Helen of Troy and Aphrodite are both depicted with red hair. The 1960s sitcom *Gilligan's Island* emphasized the glamor and sex appeal of the red-haired movie star Ginger Grant stranded on that famous island. Worldwide, less than two percent of the population has red hair naturally, with the highest density in the British Isles, at ten percent in Ireland and six percent in Scotland (Byrd).

An interesting use of the word *ginger* occurs in the mystery novel *Killing Time* by Cynthia Harrod-Eagles. When a gay singer-dancer is murdered, the police look for anyone who had met with the victim. Regarding a suspect seen with the victim at the nightclub, one detective reports: "The boss says this bloke wasn't a ginger" (86). I had to look this up. According to *Wikid-iff.com*, in UK cockney rhyming slang, ginger beer rhymes with queer. Hence, ginger means queer or homosexual, particularly male. I love finding herbal words in the language with new and surprising meanings.

Even poetry affirms ginger's legendary heat and potency. In "Poem with ginger in it", contemporary American author and ginger enthusiast Amir Majumuder affirms that eating ginger can:

Strip the paint off my throat
so that for two days, swallowing
my spit will feel like strep.

I love the pharyngeal singe.
I love the medicinal pain
that switches on a siren in my brain

and makes me pay attention
to my food.
Pepper is tepid,

cinnamon impotent.
Galangal, begone,
I'm on a binge—

it's the heat in my chai,
the kick in my Moscow Mule,
my game-changer,

game-winner,
my aspirin, my acid, my fire in winter,
my pinch of Punjab, my ginger.

Filled with magic and heat, flavor and medicine, here's to Ginger, 2023 Herb of the Year!

References

Bown, Deni. *Herbal: The Essential Guide to Herbs for Living.* Barnes & Noble, 2001. 311-313.

Byrd, Kenneth. "The Origins of Ginger Hair: Why Are Redheads Called Ginger?" *Curlcentric,* 4/10/22. https://www.curlcentric.com/why-are-redheads-called-ginger/. Accessed 10/17/22.

Castleman, Michael. *The Healing Herbs: The Ultimate Guide to the Curative Power of Nature's Medicines.* Rodale Press, 1991. 186-189.

Cunningham, Scott. *Magical Herbalism: The Secret Craft of the Wise.* Llewellyn, 1995.

----- *Cunningham's Encyclopedia of Magical Herbs.* Llewellyn, 1994.

Darazs, Margaret. "Refreshing Old-Fashioned Summer Drink: Ginger Water Plus Variations." Littlehouseontheprairie. 7/10/17. https://littlehouseontheprairie.com/refreshing-old-fashioned-summer-drink-ginger-water-recipe-plus-variations/. Accessed 9/12.22.

"Dobu Medicine." Encyclopedia.com https://www.encyclopedia.com/humanities/encyclopedias-almanacs-transcripts-and-maps/dobu. Accessed 10/21/22.

Dugan, Ellen. *Cottage Witchery: Natural Magick for Hearth and Home.* Llewellyn, 2008.

-----*Garden Witch's Herbal: Green Magick, Herbalism & Spirituality.* Llewellyn, 2009.

-----*Book of Witchery: Spells, Charms & Correspondences for Every Day of the Week.* Llewellyn, 2009.

Fulder, Stephen. *The Ginger Book: The Ultimate Home Remedy.* Avery, 1996.

"Ginger, Gingerism & Gingerphobia." *Urban Dictionary.* https://urbandictionary.com/define.php?term=Ginger. Accessed 10/29/22.

"Hansel and Gretel." *The Blue Fairy Book.* Andrew Lang, ed. Dover, 1965 (1889). 251-258.

Harrod-Eagles, Cynthia. *Killing Time.* Scribner, 1996. 86.

Hayes, Elizabeth S. *Spices and Herbs, Lore and Cookery.* Dover, 1961. 39-40.

Majmudar, Amit. "A poem with ginger in it." *Plume*, #72 July 2017. https://plumepoetry.com/poem-with-ginger-in-it/. Accessed 7/31/22.

Morrison, Dorothy. *Bud, Blossom, & Leaf.* Llewellyn, 2001.

Moore, Olivia. "Why Are Redheads Called Gingers? The Reason is Weird." YouProbablyNeedaHaircut, 8/10/22. https://youprobablyneedahaircut.com/why-are-redheads-called-gingers/. Accessed 10/17/22

Mulherin, Jennifer. *The Macmillan Treasury of Spices and Natural Flavorings.* Macmillan, 1988. 52-53.

Nicholls, Sarah. "Hansel & Gretel and the History of Gingerbread." *Another World Costumes.* https://anotherworldcostumes.com/2021/09/02/hansel-gretel-and-the-history-of-gingerbread/. Accessed 11/4/22.

Norris, Melissa. "Old-Fashioned Ginger Water Recipe (Switchel or Haymaker Punch)." https://melissaknorris.com/ginger-water/. Accessed 9/12/22.

Reader's Digest Plant Based Health Basics: Nourish Your Body & Brain with Grains, Vegetables, Beans, Nuts, and More. Reader's Digest Books, 2021.

Reppert, Bertha. *Herbs of the Zodiac.* The Rosemary House, 1984. 56-58.

Swinfen, Ann. *The Troubadour's Tale: "Historical Note."* Shakenoak Press, 2018. 271.

"The Mythology of Ginger." *Eccentric Nature.* May 16, 2021. https://www.youtube.com/watch?v=UYMKWzbm0Ps. Accessed 9/6/22.

Weiner, Michael. *Weiner's Herbal: The Guide to Herb Medicine.* Quantum, 1990. 89.

"What is the difference between homosexual and ginger?" Wikidiff. https//wikidiff.com/homosexual/ginger. Accessed 10/19/22.

Wilder, Laura Ingalls. *The Long Winter.* https://readfrom.net/laura-ingalls-wilder/33880-the_long_winter.html. Chapter 1, np.

Witchwood, Leandra. "The Magick Kitchen. Ginger: Magical Aspects, and Healing Spellwork." Witchcraft & Pagan Lifestyle Blog.
https://www.themagickkitchen.com/ginger-magickal-aspects-healing-and/. Accessed 9/6/22.

Wood, Matthew. *The Earthwise Herbal: A Complete Guide to Old World Medicinal Plants.* North Atlantic Books, 2008. 533-37.

*Retired Associate Professor of English at Middlesex County College in New Jersey, **Gert Coleman** lives on 106 hilly acres in Middlefield, New York, where she and her husband are fixing up an old house and planting herbs, flowers, trees, and at-risk native plants.*

Past president of the SI Herb Society and past board member of the International Herb Association (IHA), she edited five IHA Herb of the Year™ books (Cilantro & Coriander; Hops: Brewing and Beyond; Agastache: Anise Hyssop, Hummingbird Mints and More; Rubus and Parsley), and frequently writes about the legends, lore, and poetry of herbs.

A member of the American Botanical Council, North East Herbal Association, United Plants Savers, and the Herb Society of America, she is currently co-chair of the Cooperstown Garden Discussion Group. In addition, she offers zoom talks on all aspects of herbs, nature walks, and nature writing workshops in the wild places of New York and beyond. Gertc3456@gmail.com.

GINGER ~ A SPICY HISTORY

Karen O'Brien

Ginger (*Zingiber officinale*), a spice revered for centuries, has been cultivated for so long that it is no longer found in the wild. It has been an important ingredient for over 5,000 years in herbal medicine, relieving chills, aiding digestion, combatting flatulence, and as an aid to revive sex drive. It also acts as an antioxidant, slowing the rate at which fats combine with oxygen causing rancidity.

Ginger is thought to have been used by the Babylonians, as it is mentioned several times in the Talmud. The ancient Greeks and Romans were familiar with ginger, predating records in China and India, where much of this spice has been grown. Records of Vedic literature in India include *Atharva Veda*, written in 2000 BC, in which over 700 plants, including ginger, were listed as important in Ayurvedic healing.

The book *The Yellow Emperor's Classic of Internal Medicine*, written around 1000 BC, is the first written record of Chinese principles of health and remedies, and includes ginger among many other plants. Curiously, ginger is mentioned in the Quran as a drink of

Paradise, but it is the only plant listed in the Quran that is not also mentioned in the Bible.

Eastern medicine claims ginger as a metabolism booster; according to Western thought, ginger is useful to stimulate digestion, prevent nausea, and relieve cold symptoms. It surely stimulates pain receptors in the skin and mucous membranes—akin to the "hot" of spicy foods. Cleopatra supposedly used this spice in a love potion to woo Marc Antony, along with nutmeg and mace.

Roman emperor Mithridates VI Eupator (135 to 65 BC), King of Pontus, suspected he was being poisoned when his food began to taste strange to him. A potion, called Mithradatium, consisting of 36 ingredients, including ginger, frankincense, cinnamon, and myrrh, was created for him. By increasing his dose, he believed he developed a tolerance to poison and would not succumb. Unfortunately for him, when he was deposed and no longer wished to live, he could not drink a potion to kill himself and was forced to die by sword.

This powerful spice has long been coveted as an important essence in trade among the spice trade routes. In 110 AD, Chinese ginger was transported by caravan and traded for gold, silver, and precious gems. By 200 AD, the Romans, so desirous of this spice, were charged a tax on ginger. The Silk Road, which began as an important land route between east and west in 500 AD, originally carried precious silk. The spice trade became more lucrative and continued until 1650 AD when sea routes came into use.

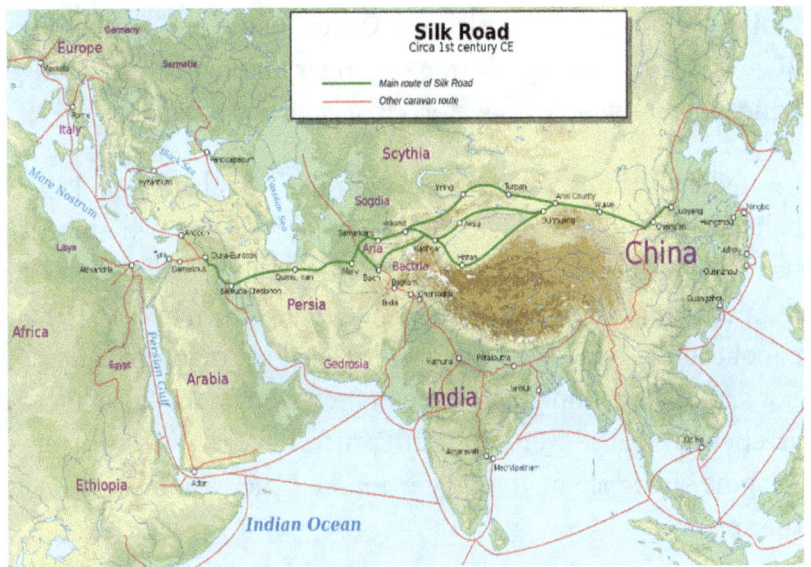

The Silk Trade Routes, both overland and maritime, in the first century AD.
Wikimedia Commons

Marco Polo was the first person to traverse the entire Silk Road, where he saw ginger being cultivated circa 1280. By the 10th century, exotic spices were being traded in Mainz, Germany, brought there by Jewish traders. Ginger's use was so widespread that it was set out on the dinner table as salt and pepper are today.

It only took another 100 years to become well known in England, as Crusaders traded with Arab merchants and brought this spice back home. One pound of ginger could be traded for a sheep —making this a very costly commodity. Crystallizing ginger, whereby sugar is added to slices of ginger to produce a sweet, became common in the 14th century when sugar became widely available.

Jubilee Pop, created to celebrate Queen Victoria's Diamond Jubilee in 1897, is a combination of ginger and lemon and orange liqueurs, combined with water, citric acid and rosewater.

In medieval times, ginger was often used to flavor ale. It was believed that ginger originated in the Garden of Eden—a beneficial plant to please mankind. By the 1800s, during times of temperance, ginger beer was created as an alternative to the alcoholic ales. Today, we have ginger ale, albeit many varieties do not actually contain ginger. The first chewing gum—also known as chewing balls—were gum of spruce flavored with ginger. I imagine the spice of the ginger masked the resinous flavor of the spruce.

Ginger is used often in cooking as an enhancement or to add some zip to cakes, cookies, breads, and other treats. The gingerbread man—a story loved by children—has a long culinary history. It was said to be devised by a baker from Rhodes in ancient Greece. The Romans then took it to Britain where it was baked in monasteries before becoming the sweet treat it is today. Queen Elizabeth I (r. 1558-1603) raised gingerbread's status when she had her baker create gingerbread portraits of honored guests and courtiers. Peter the Great, at his birth in 1672, was celebrated with a 150-pound gingerbread modeled in the shape of the Kremlin to recognize the great occasion. Who knew the gingerbread man had such a royal background!

Ginger was sometimes used in spells and rituals. Ginger was believed to increase wealth—its musky and earthy aroma, combined with sandalwood, vetiver, nutmeg, galangal, must have smelled great, too. A Hoodoo formula called VanVan brings palmarosa, citronella, lemongrass, vetiver, and ginger together for scent and spiritual power.

The term "ginger" has been applied unfairly to red-haired people, since it was believed that red hair indicated a hot temperament. And some use "ginger up" to indicate liven up or rile up. In India, it was considered a protection against disease.

However you use ginger—for cooking, medicinally, or as a sweet candy—you are following traditions of thousands of years. I always have a couple of rhizomes in my freezer, as I find that fresh grated ginger adds a little "spice" to my sauces, stir fries, and even drinks. And maybe this year, I'll make gingerbread people that look like those I love and hold dear. A new tradition, and a tasty one!

References

Bird, Stephanie Rose. *Sticks, Stones, Roots & Bones*. Llewellyn Publications, 2004.

Duff, Gail. *A Book of Herbs & Spices: Recipes, Remedies and Lore*. Salem House Publishers, 1987.

Ferry-Swainson, Kate. *Ginger*. Journey Editions, 2000.

Liebman, Malvinia. *From Caravan to Casserole: Herbs and Spices in Legend, History, and Recipes*. E.A. Seeman Publishing, 1977.

Miloradovich, Milo. *The Home Garden Book of Herbs and Spices*. Doubleday & Co., Inc., 1952.

Musselman, Lytton. *Figs, Dates, Laurel, and Myrrh: Plants of the Bible and the Quran*. Timber Press. 2007.

Norman, Jill. *The Complete Book of Spices: A Practical Guide to Spices & Aromatic Seeds*. Penguin Group, 1991.

Rinzler, Carol Ann. *The Complete Book of Herbs, Spices and Condiments*. MUF Books, 1990.

Karen O'Brien *runs her herbal business "The Green Woman's Garden" in the southwestern NH town of Richmond. She grows herbs, native plants, heirloom vegetables, and ornamental flowers, runs workshops on various herbal adventures, and is a participant in the Farmers Market in Richmond. She has gardened for more than 40 years and is certified as a Master Gardener. Karen has served on the boards of The Herb Society of America, the International Herb Association, The New England Unit of The Herb Society, and the Greenleaf Garden Club. She has edited and written for several HOY™ books, and currently writes a column for the <u>Richmond Rooster.</u>*

Spices and spice jars.
Karen O'Brien

North American wild ginger. Botanical illustration by W.J. Hooker, Royal Horticultural Society, 1827.

Asarum canadense, Curtis Botanical Magazine. plantillustrations.org

WILD GINGER
with PIPEVINE
SWALLOWTAIL
LARVA

Deborah Melia Hall 2022

TAKE A WALK ON THE WILD
SIDE WITH THE OTHER GINGER

Deborah Hall & Susan Belsinger

Although *Asarum* spp. are referred to as wild ginger, they are neither a member of, nor related to, Zingiberaceae.

Family: Aristolochiaceae; Birthwort family
Genus: *Asarum* (ah-SAR-um)
Species: *A. canadense* (American)—we are concentrating on this deciduous, Canadian wild ginger—though mention *A. europaeum* (European)
Common names: Indian Ginger, Snakeroot, Canada Snakeroot, Vermont Snakeroot, False Coltsfoot, Asarabacca
Parts Used: mostly rhizomes, sometimes leaves
Range: Canada to South Carolina and Alabama, west to Kansas, Oklahoma and Arkansas
Zones: 3 to 8
Soil: rich, moist, full of leaf mold, somewhat acidic: pH 4.5 to 6.0
Light: shade or part shade to dense shade

Plant description: As noted by Kristine Brown in her "Wild Ginger" article: "Leaves emerge folded upon themselves. They are covered with a thick down. Keyword: Fuzzy." This creeping plant has two heart-shaped leaves on hairy stems; leaves are dark green, smooth-edged and very veiny. Single flower is hidden below, in the fork (crotch) of the leaves, at ground level. It is a curious little cup-shaped flower with three sepals in shades of reddish-brown, maroon to burgundy. The rhizome (often referred to as a root), fresh or dried, is highly aromatic with a spicy *Zingiber* scent when broken, bruised or cut. It is pungent, acrid, warming and drying to taste.

Propagation: Can be propagated by seed, cuttings or root division. Seeds can be sown about 6 weeks after flowers start to bloom. The seed needs stratification, most easily done by wintering over in the seedbed. The simplest method is from rhizomes, which can be divided in spring or fall and replanted.

Of note: Hidden flowers are pollinated by ants and beetles; slugs like to eat the leaves. Plants of the Aristolochiaceae, which include wild ginger, birthworts and pipevines (all contain aristolochic acid) are food sources for the pipevine swallowtail butterfly larvae.

Deborah has a deep woodland garden and that is where she grows *Asarum canadense*, along with Jack-in-the-Pulpit, bloodroot, hostas, hellebores, violets and ferns in moist rich soil with lots of deciduous leaf mold, beneath hardwoods like oak and hickory.

Wild ginger's heart-shaped leaves.
Susan Belsinger

She also has a large patch growing on what was the old farm road that runs through the woods. It probably came from a piece of rhizome that was dropped in the deciduous leaves while cleaning up flowerbeds. It is somewhat slow spreading, although after 20 years, the patch has expanded to about 3 x 9 feet. As a child, Deborah remembers it as a commonplace woodland plant in the old deciduous woodlots and stream bottoms on the farms in Howard County, Maryland.

This American creeping ground cover can be grown together with *Asarum europaeum,* which is a smaller plant with shiny leaves, along with other shade-loving woodland plants. Gertrude Jekyll used American wild ginger in her woodland garden with *Rhododendron, Amelanchier, Digitalis* and ferns. We often find it growing in colonies in the wild on wood walks.

Susan is fond of this ground cover and planted it right outside her backdoor in a native shade garden. Growing on the north side, and spreading a little each year, American *Asarum* has the most wonderful, deep wine-colored, fuzzy flowers beneath the heart-shaped leaves. She savors that one has to bend down and get close to the earth—really get into the midst of the plant—in order to part the leaves to see these magical, three-sepaled, cup-shaped blooms. If you do not take the time to do this—you will totally miss seeing these darling blooms under the foliage. They bloom late winter to mid-spring depending upon where you live—and the blooms last about three weeks.

Wild ginger flowers.
Pat Kenny

Garden writer Allan Armitage agrees about one's relationship with these hidden gems: "I love teaching these plants to students and guests, because to truly appreciate them, you must go down on your hands and knees, and get flower-to-eyeball."

Wild ginger plants are grown from rhizomes, which are simplest to propagate in spring or fall. When these rhizomes are bruised or chopped, they smell a lot like true ginger. In *Herbal Renaissance,* Steven Foster states: "In the nineteenth century the root was a substitute for true ginger, because of its aromatic, somewhat ginger-like fragrance. The similarities end there. The fresh roots are fun to nibble while hiking through the forest. Candy the roots as you would calamus or angelica roots."

In the past, the rhizomes of *Asarum* spp. have been used medicinally as an aid for digestion and used as a flavoring to hide the taste of other medicine, often as a cordial. Essential oils of wild gingers contain asarene, azulene, borneol, delta-linalool, eugenol, geraniol, methyl eugenol, pinenes and terpineol. Besides essential oils, they contain alkaloids, aristolochic acid, glycosides, mucilage, resin and tannins. Since this plant contains aristolochic acid it should be used or consumed only in small amounts by responsible individuals who have done their research and plant identification or used as directed by a knowledgeable health care practitioner. Aristolochic acid is considered a toxin and is carcinogenic and mutagenic. That said, experienced herbalists today use it to flavor syrups or honey, as a candied root, and formulated in tinctures, oils, and salves. There are research studies using it to lessen the occurrence of herpes lesions and as an antitumor compound.

According to Daniel Moerman in *Native American Ethnobotany*, there are a multitude of diseases and conditions that wild ginger has been used for, listed along with the Native American tribes who used them. Wild ginger was used for maladies from toothache, earache, and sore throat to respiratory ailments, gastric distress, and ptomaine poisoning, to venereal disease, female complaints and as an abortifacient. Numerous tribes like the Bella Coola, Cherokee, Chippewa, Malecite, Menominee, Meskwak, Micmac, Ojibwa, Okanagon and Thompson all used *Asarum* for gastrointestinal issues, while the Cherokee, Chippewa, Iroquois, Modesse, Pomo, Pomo Kashaya, Thompson and Yurok used it as a dermatological aid.

In the United States, the history and ongoing studies of *Asarum canadense* are similar to the related species in Europe (*Asarum europaeum*, known as asarabacca); the safety and efficacy of these botanicals need to be further studied and developed.

References

Armitage, Allan. *Armitage's Native Plants*. Timber Press, 2006. p. 53.

Benyus, Janine M. *The Field Guide to Wildlife Habitats of the Eastern United States*. Fireside, 1989.

Brown, Kristine. "Wooly Wild Ginger." *Herbal Roots Zine*, Volume 9, Issue 5, May 2017.

Elliot, Doug. *Wild Roots: A Forager's Guide to the Edible and Medicinal Roots, Tubers, Corms and Rhizomes of North America*. Healing Arts Press, 1995.

Feltwell, John. *The Naturalists Garden*. Salem House, 1987.

Foster, Steven. *Herbal Renaissance*. Gibbs-Smith, 1984.

Foster, Steven and James A. Duke. *Peterson Field Guide to Medicinal Plants and Herbs*. Houghton Mifflin Harcourt, 2014.

Moerman, Daniel. *Native American Ethnobotany*. Timber Press, 1998.

Deborah Hall, *artist, florist and gardener, loves and plays with plants and animals in Howard County, Maryland. She has been a longtime supporter of IHA's herbs of the year, sharing her plants, seeds and knowledge.*

Susan Belsinger *delights in learning, whether it is about a person, place, plant, thing, or each new herb of the year: doing research, growing the specimens, botanizing, taking photos, creating recipes, sharing her findings and celebrating the plants. Her latest book is the perfect bite: focus on flavor.*

GINGER IN THE KITCHEN

Ginger in its many forms ~ clockwise from bottom left: candied, pickled, ground, dried, fresh cut into coins, fresh grated, whole rhizome or hand.
Susan Belsinger

Pickled ginger made from just-harvested fresh rhizomes is
a mouthwatering condiment.
Susan Belsinger

GINGERY GOODIES

Susan Belsinger

Gingerroot has an assertive spiciness—first it is pungent and quite hot on the tongue—and then it is earthy, aromatic and a bit exotic, ending with some citrus notes. Ground, fresh, or candied, it is added to all sorts of beverages and libations, quick breads like muffins and scones, gingerbread, spice cakes, cookies and confections.

Although ginger's bright piquancy stands out in savory dishes, it shines in desserts and beverages. When combined with sweetener, be it sugar, molasses, honey or maple syrup, the stimulating warmth and pungency of this rhizome, whether it is freshly grated, candied, or dried and ground, results in irresistible and comforting spicy and sweet treats. Here are a few of my tried-and-true ginger recipes.

How to store and preserve the rhizomes

Once you have harvested your ginger rhizomes or brought them home from the grocery, here is how best to keep ginger. Wash the rhizomes thoroughly, air dry and then store these fresh rhizomes wrapped in a paper towel in a paper bag on the inside door of the refrigerator. Do not seal them in plastic bags as this encourages mold and will spoil the crop. Rhizomes can also be wrapped well or put into freezer containers and frozen.

Slice rhizomes and dry them in the dehydrator for fresh dried ginger (which is much more flavorful than the powdered that you buy in the store) and grate it on a grater as you would nutmeg for a fresh ground spice. My favorite way to preserve ginger is in the following recipe for pickled ginger.

Pungent Pickled Ginger

This pickled ginger is easy to make and so much better than what you buy in jars at the store. It is fresh and a tad crunchy and quite zingy with pungency. It makes quite a bit of juice which is great to use in salad dressings, dipping sauces and marinades. I've been making pickled ginger for quite a long time—it is so worth the time and effort. This recipe is adapted from Barbara Tropp's China Moon Cookbook, Workman Publishing, 1992. Her original recipe uses three kinds of vinegar—I combine Japanese rice vinegar with apple cider vinegar (which adds a little more acid tang)—however using all rice vinegar works too.

I am so very fortunate that my daughter Lucie and her husband Matt, grow the most amazing organic ginger on their Harbinger Farm in Myrtle Creek, Oregon. Their newly harvested ginger is primo—it has purplish-pink buds and is tender with no internal fibers and does not need to be peeled—it is still very pungent and makes the most amazing pickled ginger. That said, grocery store ginger with tannish-brown skin still works perfectly well.

Choose firm-textured fresh ginger without any mold or soft spots. Wash the ginger root well. The ginger can be peeled with a vegetable peeler, paring knife, spoon, or a grapefruit spoon removes the thin skin easily.

(Note: I save these peelings and decoct them in a saucepan with 3 or 4 cups water for about 20 minutes. Stir in a scant cup of organic sugar, or to taste, until dissolved or leave the decoction unsweetened. Cover and let cool to room temperature, then strain into a jar and refrigerate; use the ginger syrup to make ginger ale or add to tea or other beverages.)

After peeling, the fibrous rhizomes must be sliced crosswise to make thin coins; they should be nearly paper thin, so a mandolin or the Benriner (a Japanese version which is much less expensive—available at Asian markets or online) make this job quick and easy—or a very sharp knife with a thin blade and patience to slice the ginger very thinly will work.

Makes about a quart

> A generous 1-pound fresh ginger root
> About 3 cups boiling water
> 4 to 6 red shiso (perilla) leaves, optional
> About 3 cups rice vinegar (unseasoned)
> 1 cup organic sugar
> 2 1/2 tablespoons sea salt
> 1/3 cup apple cider vinegar

Put the paper-thin-sliced ginger coins into a bowl and pour the boiling water over the ginger; let stand for 2 or 3 minutes and then drain in a large strainer or colander. Transfer the ginger into a clean quart jar. Tuck the shiso leaves amongst the ginger slices, if using them.

In a non-reactive saucepan, combine the rice vinegar, sugar and salt. Heat gently and stir until the sugar and salt dissolve; do not simmer or boil. Remove from heat and stir in the apple cider vinegar; pour the vinegar mixture over the prepared ginger in the jar.

Let the contents of the jar cool to room temperature. Cover with a plastic lid and refrigerate. The ginger can be used after 24 hours; however, I like it better after a week or two. It will keep for several months in refrigerator.

Award-Winning Ginger Vanilla Bean Elixir

This syrup won First Place in the Best Syrup or Elixir category at the 2009 International Herb Symposium! It is warming and stimulating and very good for a sore throat, cold or flu. The lemon herbs are optional; however, I use them whenever I can add them fresh since they add a subtle yet enchanting lemon-sweet bouquet.

The syrup makes an exceptional homemade ginger ale; just fill a glass partway with ice, then add ginger syrup to about halfway and top off the other half with sparkling water, stir and enjoy. If you add a shot of dark rum and a wedge of lime, you'll have a delightful libation that I call a Humdinger Rum Zinger! Excerpted from <u>the perfect bite: focus on flavor</u>.

Makes about 4 cups

    4 cups water
    7- to 8-inch piece ginger root, peeled and cut into 'coins' (about 2 cups)
    2 cups raw, organic sugar
    1/2 vanilla bean, split lengthwise
    1/2 lime or lemon, sliced; sometimes I use just the zest
    Handful of fresh lemon verbena, lemon basil or lemon balm leaves, optional

To make this herb syrup, the gingerroot must be decocted first. Put the water in a small saucepan, place over moderate heat and bring to a boil. Add the ginger coins and vanilla bean, reduce heat, and simmer gently for about 20 minutes. Stir the sugar in to dissolve it, add the lime or lemon and the lemon herbs, cover and let stand for least 30 minutes, or until room temperature.

Once cooled to room temperature, strain, and refrigerate. (If you are in a hurry, sit the hot pan of syrup in an ice bath to cool it quickly.) This syrup can be made ahead and kept in the refrigerator for about 2 weeks. Be sure to label, because all of the syrups look similar. Store for up to a year in the freezer (be sure to leave plenty of headspace).

creative possibilities

Δ *If you don't have a vanilla bean—which is truly what makes this syrup ethereal—you can add a few teaspoons pure vanilla extract after it has cooled.*

Δ *I have made this with both maple syrup and honey—they are both good—however their flavors tend to dominate.*

Δ *Toss with fruit salad, drizzle over pancakes, waffles or ice cream.*

Δ *It is delicious stirred into tea, mixed with lemonade or with other juices to make a tasty beverage or fruit punch and is one of my favorite flavorings for water kefir.*

Δ *I use this with sparkling water over ice for a lovely mocktail. I also use it like ginger beer—it is particularly good in a Moscow mule (or any mule from vodka to whiskey); add a shot to your next mojito!*

Triple-Gingery Gingerbread

This gingerbread is very gingery with a trio of ginger preparations: ground, fresh grated and candied. I make it with just 1/3 cup brown sugar—though it is not very sweet—so if you prefer it cakey-sweet then add the 1/2 cup. For breakfast, I like it smeared with cream cheese and anytime with my homemade applesauce.

Also, sorghum molasses versus unsulfured molasses is very distinct— sorghum is sweeter and will make a golden-brown-colored gingerbread, whereas unsulfured molasses is a tad bitter, stronger in flavor and will make a much darker cake. Both are delectable, just elicit different results. Excerpted from <u>the perfect bite: focus on flavor</u>.

Makes 8-inch pan gingerbread; cut into 16 or 20 pieces

   1 cup unbleached flour
   2/3 cup whole wheat pastry flour
   1 teaspoon baking powder
   1/2 teaspoon salt
   2 1/2 teaspoons ground ginger
   Generous 1/4 teaspoon ground mace
   Generous 1/4 teaspoon ground cloves
   1/4 teaspoon ground mustard
   6 tablespoons unsalted butter, softened
   1/3 to 1/2 cup dark brown sugar
   2 extra-large eggs
   1/2 cup sorghum or unsulfured molasses
   2/3 cup just-boiled water
   1 teaspoon baking soda
   1 1/2 tablespoons grated peeled ginger root
   About 2 tablespoons crystallized ginger, finely chopped

Preheat the oven to 350°F. Butter an 8-inch square baking pan.

In a medium bowl, sift the flours, baking powder, salt, ground ginger, mace, cloves, and mustard.

In a large bowl, cream the butter with the brown sugar and add the eggs one at a time and mix well to combine.

Measure the sorghum or molasses into a large heat-proof measuring cup, pour in the just-boiled water and stir with a spoon to dissolve the molasses. Stir in the baking soda (which will bubble up) and then add the fresh grated ginger and candied ginger pieces, stir to combine.

Add the flour mixture to the creamed butter in three batches, alternating with the molasses mixture in two parts until just blended. Pour the batter into the prepared pan. Bake about 30 minutes or until a cake tester comes out clean. Cool in the pan on a rack until just warm or room temperature before cutting into squares.

creative possibilities

Δ *Options are to make this a little less sweet or sweeter. If you are serving it with a sweet topping like whipped cream, ice cream or lemon curd, it needn't be too sweet.*

Δ *If eating plain or with unsweetened yogurt or applesauce, perhaps you'd like it a tad sweeter.*

Δ *Unsulfured molasses is less sweet than sorghum molasses.*

Δ *Use all unbleached flour for a lighter cake.*

Triple -Gingery Gingerbread is especially good served with Homemade Applesauce with Cider.
Susan Belsinger

Maple Scones with Ginger and Lemon Verbena

You can substitute any lemon herb in these scones; orange mint is also delicious. Of course, using fresh herbs will give you the most wonderful bouquet in addition to flavor. However, you may use dried herbs if need be—reduce the amount of dried herbs to about 2 tablespoons—and stir it into the milk and let stand for about 10 to 15 minutes. The scones can be prepared with all unbleached flour, which will make them a bit lighter, the whole-wheat flour makes them a bit more toothsome.

Makes about 1 dozen scones

1 1/2 cups unbleached white flour
1 cup whole-wheat flour

1 teaspoon ground ginger
3/4 teaspoon salt
3 teaspoons baking powder
8 tablespoons cold, unsalted butter, cut into pieces
3/4 cup milk or buttermilk
1/4 cup + 1 tablespoon pure maple syrup
About 3 to 4 tablespoons freshly chopped lemon verbena
1/4 cup finely chopped candied ginger

Preheat oven to 425ºF. Combine the flours, ginger, salt, and baking powder in a large bowl and blend thoroughly. Cut in the butter until the mixture resembles a coarse meal.

Stir the milk, 1/4 cup of the syrup, and the lemon verbena together. Add the liquid to the dry ingredients and stir to form a soft dough.

Turn the dough onto a floured pastry marble or board, knead gently with a few turns, until it just comes together. Roll the dough out into a circular shape, about 3/4-inch thick. Brush the top of the dough with the remaining tablespoon of maple syrup. Cut the dough into 8 or 12 wedges with a sharp knife or pizza cutter and place on an ungreased baking sheet.

Bake the scones for 18 to 20 minutes or until golden brown. Remove to baking rack to cool slightly before serving. The scones are best served warm and right after baking.

If you want to prepare them in advance, cool them completely and store them in an airtight container. Wrap them in foil and gently reheat them in a 325ºF degree oven for about 10 to 15 minutes.

Triple Ginger Snaps with Sorghum

These ginger snaps are extra pungent with ginger since they have Zingiber officinale in three different forms: ground, candied, and fresh grated root. The sorghum syrup combines well to make a flavorful cookie.

Makes about 4 dozen

2 1/4 cups unbleached flour
1 teaspoon baking powder
1/2 teaspoon salt
2 teaspoons ground ginger
2 tablespoons finely chopped candied ginger
1 cup unsalted butter, softened
1 cup brown sugar
1/3 cup sorghum
2 extra-large eggs
1 tablespoon freshly grated ginger root
1 teaspoon pure vanilla extract
About 1/3 cup sugar

Preheat oven to 350ºF. In a bowl combine the dry ingredients: flour, baking powder, salt, ground ginger and candied ginger; toss well to mix.

In a food processor or a mixer, pulse or cream butter with the brown sugar until fluffy. Add the sorghum and mix until combined. Add the eggs, one at a time, until mixed; add the gingerroot and vanilla extract and pulse or mix until combined. Add the dry ingredients and pulse or mix until just blended.

Place the sugar in a saucer. Scoop the dough by the heaping tea-spoonful and roll into balls. Roll each ball in the sugar to coat and place them on a baking sheet at least 2 inches apart.

Bake in a preheated oven for 10 to 12 minutes until flattened and cracked on top. Remove the pan from the oven and let the cookies stand for about 2 minutes. Remove cookies from the pan onto baking racks to cool. Store in a tightly closed tin for up to a week or freeze for up to 3 months.

Ginger has been dried and ground and used in recipes for thousands of years. If you dry your own ginger slices, you can grate them fresh (like nutmeg) into your recipes. Freshly ground dried ginger is very flavorful.

Susan Belsinger

Grated fresh ginger is a great way
to get its pungent flavor into a dish.

A simple box grater will do the job and a microplane is a
handy tool; however, this special ginger grater does a fine
job, and it contains the grated rhizome in the bottom
compartment for easy measurement and clean up.
Susan Belsinger

COOKING WITH GINGER

Gert Coleman

Ginger has always been part of my life. At home, we drank flat ginger ale to cure an upset stomach, and my father, a nurse, applied hot ginger-mustard plasters to "break up" rheumy chest colds. I read and reread the Little House books—much of my agricultural knowledge comes from them—and I always remembered Ma's ginger water. As a teacher, I drank hot ginger tea when I was losing my voice, and when students were coughing and sneezing in my confined classroom, I went home and ate ginger-garlic honey. Lately, I've discovered Manuka honey drops loaded with grated ginger for when my throat feels dry or, in these Covid times, when I've been shopping or hobnobbing with too many people.

In a variety of forms, ginger can add both spice and health to almost any meal, brightening soups, vegetables, and coffee cakes. Ginger's far-reaching culinary appeal can enhance any dish from soup to nuts.

Soothing Ginger Root Tea

According to herbal wisdom, drink ginger beverages if you are always cold. Ginger also warms the stomach to improve digestion. Should you peel your ginger? According to food historian Pat Crocker, not if it's organic ginger, but non-organic ginger should always be peeled. As a teacher, losing my voice in the classroom was disastrous. One semester, a Chinese student gave me this recipe. After drinking a cup or two, I regained my voice and felt much better. Now I make it at the first sign of respiratory trouble. I use about an inch of ginger, and slice carefully or chop indiscriminately, depending on how I feel.

Yields 4 cups

> 1-inch piece fresh ginger, thinly sliced or grated
> 4 cups water
> 1 to 2 teaspoons honey
> Slice of lemon or 1/2 teaspoon lemon juice

Wash ginger and slice thinly or grate. In a saucepan, cover ginger with 4 cups of water and bring to a boil. Simmer gently, uncovered, for 20 to 30 minutes. The longer you simmer it, the "hotter" the taste of the ginger will be. Strain. Stir in honey and add a squeeze of lemon. Drink warm. Refrigerate any leftovers.

Garlic-Ginger Honey

A dip, a condiment, or an immune-booster—you decide! I made this once for a class on ginger and served it with crackers. I had none left to bring home, it was that popular! Delicious on chicken or vegetables, or straight off the spoon.

Yields 2 to 4 servings

2 ounces honey
1 to 2 cloves garlic, minced
1/2-inch piece ginger, minced or grated
Dash cayenne pepper, optional

In a pretty glass dish, pour honey, then add ginger and garlic. Mix well and serve at room temperature.

Ginger-Scallion Soup

This clear, tasty soup makes an easy first course for a dinner party. Top with parsley for extra nutrition. It is also a quick and easy soup to sip at the first sign of illness.

Yields 4 servings

3 to 4 scallions thinly sliced
2 teaspoons freshly grated ginger root
4 cups water

Bring water to a boil in a saucepan and add scallions and ginger. Simmer over low heat, partly covered, about 15 minutes. Serve in bowls.

Baked Butternut Squash with Ginger and Cranberries

Butternut squash baked with butter and local maple syrup is an autumnal delight, but it really soars with ginger and cranberries. Measurement of ingredients is approximate depending on the size of your squash. This can be a meal unto itself, or an accompaniment to roast pork or poultry. Substitute chopped apple or peach for the cranberries, if you like, and add a dash of allspice, clove, mace, or cardamom.

Yields 2 servings

1 butternut squash, halved lengthwise, seeds removed
4 tablespoons butter
2 to 4 tablespoons fresh cranberries, enough to fill each cavity
1/2 teaspoon cinnamon
1 teaspoon minced crystallized or 1/2 teaspoon ground ginger
2 tablespoons maple syrup or brown sugar
Salt and pepper, optional

Preheat oven to 400ºF. Prepare squash halves by removing seeds and pulp. With the tines of a fork, poke lines down and across the top of the squash.

Fill cavities with butter, cranberries, cinnamon, ginger, and maple syrup. Place face up on a cookie sheet or roasting pan and bake for about an hour, until the squash is tender.

Butternut-Apple Soup with Ginger

Butternut squash has an affinity with ginger, maybe because they are both sweet and warming. You can halve and roast the squash, then scoop the flesh into the soup pot, or you can peel, cube, and cook along with the other ingredients. It's delicious either way. I prefer tart apples like Granny Smith, but any apples will work. Serve with croutons, pepitas, or sliced scallion rings.

Yields 6 servings

1 butternut squash
2 tablespoons butter or olive oil
1 small onion, minced
1 stalk celery, minced

2 carrots, minced
2 quarts chicken or vegetable stock
2 apples, peeled, cored, and diced
1 teaspoon grated fresh or 1/2 teaspoon ground ginger
1/4 teaspoon cayenne or Hungarian paprika
1/2 teaspoon cinnamon
Dash white pepper

You can use either roasted squash or fresh squash, cubed. If roasting, halve the squash lengthwise and roast in a 400ºF oven for 30 to 40 minutes, or until tender.

Remove from oven and allow to cool. Scoop the flesh into a bowl and set aside. Discard the peel. If using fresh squash, peel and cube the squash and set aside.

In a soup pot, melt butter and add onion, celery, and carrots. Sauté until tender, then add cubed or roasted squash and stock and simmer for 20 minutes. Add chopped apple and ginger and simmer another 20 minutes. Add cayenne or paprika and cinnamon, and simmer for 5 minutes.

Then blend, using an immersion blender, until smooth. Taste and correct for seasonings.

Cantonese-Style Steamed Fish with Ginger and Scallions

My good friend Skye Suter loves fish and gave me this recipe last summer. According to Skye, "Steaming is a great way to cook a whole fish or a piece of fish to succulent perfection. The freshest whole fish will have clear eyes, firm flesh, and red gills. A piece of fish should look firm and glossy. Some fish that are good to steam include cod, grouper, snapper, sea bass, halibut or Branzino (aka European bass.) This recipe is for whole fish but a thick fish steak can be substituted if desired. Have the proprietor clean the fish for you—it's a messy job to do at home. They will scale and gut it and remove the head if you want. We like to leave the head on. It makes a nicer presentation." I leave the head off, but add plenty of ginger and scallions.

Yields 4 servings

2 whole fish, cleaned and gutted
3 or 4 1-inch knobs of ginger, peeled and cut into slivers
4 to 6 scallions cut into 1/4-inch lengths, reserve half
4 tablespoons soy sauce
1 to 2 tablespoons sesame oil

Cut 2 or 3 slits into the sides of the fish and insert ginger, then tuck the rest of the ginger and half the scallions inside of the fish. If you have a fish poacher, steam the fish on top of the stove. Just make sure that both fish fit into the poacher at the same time. If a poacher is not handy, a roasting pan may be used.

Fish Poacher Method: Place some water in the bottom of poacher, almost to the level of the steaming rack, then turn the stove to medium high heat. When the water comes to a boil, place the fish on the rack, cover, reduce heat, and steam 10 minutes. Test for doneness, then steam for a couple minutes longer, if needed.

Roasting Pan Method: Preheat oven to 450ºF. Fit a wire rack into a roasting pan. Add water to the bottom of the pan, almost to the level of the rack. Wrap the fish in parchment paper, folding over to make a package. Place the fish on the rack and cover the roasting pan with foil. Turn temperature down to 400ºF. Steam for 10 minutes and test for doneness, then steam for a couple minutes longer, if needed.

To test for doneness: When fish is properly cooked the flesh becomes more opaque and loses the translucency of fresh fish and the flesh is firmer to the touch. When you take it out of the steamer, the residual heat will still cook the fish a bit more. Do not overcook.

With a fish spatula, gently remove the fish to a serving platter. Sprinkle the other half of the scallions over the fish. Stir the soy sauce and sesame oil together then pour over the fish. Serve immediately.

Blueberry-Ginger Kaffee Kuchen

When I came across blueberry-ginger crumb cake squares at a local co-op, I determined to make this at home. But the how, when, and what form of ginger to use mystified me. Consulting with Susan Belsinger, I learned that creative cooks can sprinkle freshly grated ginger, finely minced crystallized ginger, or powdered ginger over the fruit. I really like blueberries mixed with blackberries, but apples, peaches, pears, nectarines, and or raspberries also pair well with ginger.

And what about ginger in the cake or the crumb topping? Ultimately, I prefer the simple surprise of ginger in the fruit layer, with a golden cake underneath and a traditional crumb topping above. For those who love the burst of ginger in every bite, Susan suggests adding up to a teaspoon of ground ginger to the cake batter, and at least a quarter teaspoon to the topping for a truly gingery experience. Either way, definitely try adding ginger to your next coffee cake. Delicious on its own, or even better with vanilla ice cream or whipped cream.

Yields 16 servings

Spicy Topping

1/2 cup brown sugar

2 tablespoons flour

1 teaspoon ground cinnamon

1/4 teaspoon ground ginger, optional

3/4 cup chopped walnuts

2 tablespoons melted butter

In a glass bowl, combine brown sugar, flour, cinnamon, ginger, walnuts, and butter and set aside. This can be made ahead of time and kept in the refrigerator till ready to be used.

Fruit layer

1 cup blueberries, or 1/2 cup each blueberries and blackberries

1 teaspoon minced crystallized, or 1 tablespoon freshly grated ginger

1 tablespoon flour

In another glass bowl, combine blueberries with minced ginger and flour and toss gently. Set aside. Drain off any liquid before adding to cake.

Cake

1/2 cup flour

2 teaspoons baking powder

1/2 teaspoon salt

1/2 cup butter, softened

3/4 cup sugar

2 egg yolks

1/2 cup milk
2 stiffly beaten egg whites

Preheat oven to 350ºF. Grease a 9 x 9 x 2-inch pan.

For the cake, sift together the dry ingredients: flour, baking powder and salt and set aside. Cream together butter and sugar. Beat in the egg yolks. Add the dry ingredients in two parts alternately with the milk, beating well after each addition. Fold in egg whites and pour batter into prepared pan.

Add blueberry mixture, pressing in slightly, then sprinkle the spicy topping evenly over the cake. Bake for 30 to 45 minutes, until a skewer inserted comes out clean.

Rosemary-Ginger Walnuts

Based on Betsy Williams' recipe in <u>Mrs. Thrift Cooks</u>, which was based on Emelie Tolley's recipe, this delightful canapé has made the rounds of herbal gatherings for decades. In my version, ginger's sweet spicy flavor blends well with cayenne and rosemary. Any paprika will do but a smoky Spanish paprika takes it to a new level. Excellent as an appetizer, chopped to top vegetables, salads, or shortbread cookies, as a garnish to meats and fish. Bag with a ribbon and give as gifts.

2 to 3 tablespoons butter
2 tablespoons extra virgin olive oil
1 pound walnut halves
2 1/2 teaspoons chive or garlic salt
1 teaspoon paprika
2 to 3 tablespoons dried rosemary
Dash or two cayenne pepper
1 to 2 teaspoons powdered ginger

Preheat oven to 325ºF, then heat butter and oil in a roasting pan. Add nuts to the pan and stir to cover with butter and oil. Scatter the salt, paprika, rosemary, cayenne, and ginger over the nuts and stir again. Spread nuts into a single layer and place pan in oven. Roast for 20 to 25 minutes, shaking the pan and stirring the nuts every few minutes to prevent burning. Do not overcook.

When golden brown and toasted, spread nuts on paper towels to cool and dry. Taste and add more salt and rosemary if needed. Pack in zip-close bags and store in freezer till needed.

Ginger rhizome watercolor.
Gail Wood Miller

SOME FAMILY FAVORITE
GINGER RECIPES

Kathleen Connole

Baked Sweet Potatoes and Apples with Ginger and Vanilla Bourbon Cranberry Sauce

This recipe was original to my mother-in-law, Wuanita Connole, and she always made it simply, with butternut squash, instead of the sweet potatoes, and apples, which is also delicious. I added ginger to the recipe in celebration of Ginger as Herb of the Year. If cranberries are not in season, dried cranberries or cherries can be sprinkled on top before serving.

Yields 8 to 10 servings

4 to 6 sweet potatoes, peeled and sliced
4 tart apples, peeled and sliced
6 tablespoons unsalted butter
3 tablespoons unbleached all-purpose flour
1/2 cup brown sugar

1 tablespoon fresh ginger, grated
1 teaspoon ground dried ginger
1/2 teaspoon salt

Prepare sweet potatoes and apples, place in a buttered 9 x 13-inch pan. Preheat oven to 350ºF.

Melt butter in heavy-bottomed saucepan, add sugar and salt; stir until dissolved. Add flour, stir to blend.

Sprinkle ginger over sweet potatoes and apples.

Pour butter-sugar mixture over sweet potatoes and apples, cover pan with foil. Bake for 45 minutes, or until sweet potatoes and apples are tender. Remove foil for last few minutes of baking.

Vanilla Bourbon Cranberry Sauce

This year at Thanksgiving our niece served this Vanilla Bourbon Cranberry Sauce which was a big hit. The recipe came from Pinterest and the person who posted it said she had no idea where it came from; she found it scribbled on a post-it in her husband's folder of favorite recipes. An internet search revealed several versions, often including orange juice and zest. I reduced the sugar amount called for from 1 cup to 1/2 cup, and it is still plenty sweet. Maple syrup could be used instead. The natural pectin in the cranberries will thicken the sauce.

For a winter solstice potluck, I decided to drizzle the sauce over the sweet potato and apple dish. This will be our new favorite when cranberries are in season. It is a simple and delicious accompaniment to the traditional Thanksgiving dinner.

12 ounces fresh cranberries, washed
1/2 cup raw sugar
1 cup water
1 vanilla bean, split, or 1 tablespoon pure vanilla extract
2 tablespoons bourbon

Place cranberries, water, sugar, vanilla bean and bourbon in a heavy-bottomed saucepan. Bring to a boil; reduce heat and simmer on medium heat for 15 to 20 minutes, stirring often. If using vanilla extract, add after removing from heat. Cool. Sauce thickens as it cools.

Drizzle over sweet potatoes and apples before serving.

Baked Sweet Potatoes and Apples with Ginger and Cranberries is a delicious Thanksgiving side dish.
Kathleen Connole

Ginger Syrup with Coconut Sugar, Vanilla, and Cardamom

This ginger syrup uses coconut sugar as an alternative to regular sugar. I prefer it because it has a lower glycemic index. Real vanilla bean and cardamom are delicious compliments to the spiciness of the ginger. Sugar amount can be adjusted, according to your taste preference.

Yields 2 cups

   2 cups fresh (peeled if needed) ginger root, sliced into coins
   2 cups spring water
   1 cup coconut sugar
   1 vanilla bean, split open
   2 teaspoons crushed cardamom seed
   Fresh lemon slices, optional

Place ginger, water, coconut sugar, vanilla bean, and cardamom in a saucepan. Gently simmer over medium heat for 30 minutes. Cool and strain into a glass jar. Keep refrigerated for up to one month. It will keep in the freezer for several months.

Add one or two tablespoons of this syrup to a glass of ice; add chilled plain or naturally citrus-flavored sparkling water. A twist of lemon can also be added, if desired.

Ingredients for Ginger Syrup with Vanilla Bean and Cardamom.
Kathleen Connole

References

"Vanilla Bourbon Cranberry Sauce." https://werefarfrom-normal.com. Accessed 2-22-23.

Freshly sliced ginger root.
Susan Belsinger

GOOD, GREAT, GULP-ABLE GINGER

Pat Crocker

Ginger, as Dioscorides reporteth, is right good with meat
in sauces, or otherwise in conditures:
for it is of an heating and digesting qualitie,
and is profitable for the stomache,
and effectually opposeth it selfe against all darkness
of the sight; answering the qualities and effects of Pepper.
–Gerard [1]

The dried root of Ginger (*Zingiber officinale*) has been used "as a condiment and aromatic stimulant from ancient times"[2]. And from the fifteenth century, ginger was exported from Zanzibar—a possible origin of the Latin, *Zingiber*—for use by healers, monks and herbalists in syrup, tincture, and other carminative simples.

The tradition of flavouring drinks with ginger may have originated long before the seventeen hundreds but we do know that in England, from around the middle of the 18th century, ginger was fermented with sugar, water, and a starter culture to make an alcoholic beverage that quenched thirst and quelled stomachs at the same time. That drink was called *ginger beer* and it has survived—with and without alcohol—right up to the present time.

Almost a century later (1890 to be precise), an enterprising Canadian chemist, John McLaughlin began bottling his own soda water. Never one to coast, McLaughlin's experiments with natural flavourings and recipes led him to his greatest accomplishment, Canada Dry® Pale Ginger Ale, invented in 1904. Originally made with real ginger, Canada Dry Ginger Ale was designed as a non-alcoholic, refreshing drink but it also became a perfect bedside anti-emetic as well as a mixer for alcoholic drinks.

Anti-emetic? Ginger root is used as a natural remedy for nausea and vomiting, which is why many people of my generation actually remember being given a serving of flat ginger ale if we were sick with the flu. Ginger ale was decanted to a glass and set aside to rest until all of the bubbles disappeared, leaving a sweet, ginger-flavoured liquid that was effective in calming upset tummies. Today, this isn't possible because Canada Dry® Ginger Ale does not list ginger in the ingredients.

Fast-forward to 2023 and the recent "discovery" and excitement around fermented foods, which fostered a modern take on historic ginger beer or ginger ale drinks. It's called *Ginger Bug* (recipe follows) and is made by combining grated fresh ginger with a small amount of sugar and water. Sound familiar? The now popular Ginger Bug drink is actually Ginger Beer; however, while it *is* fermented, it contains no significant amount of alcohol.

We've been taking good, great gulps of ginger for medicine, as a thirst-quencher, and to mix with alcoholic spirits for a very long time. What follows is a clutch of non-alcoholic beverages that pair ginger with popular flavour affiliates such as lemon, carrot, chocolate, cream, apples, cider vinegar, honey, pears, rhubarb, peaches, and mint.

Ginger Bug

Bugs (bacteria) make this drink probiotic. It uses friendly bacteria, similar to bacteria that are already inside your body, especially your gut, to produce a slightly sour-tasting, naturally carbonated drink. Probiotics boost the immune system, prevent and help heal urinary tract infections, improve digestion, and help treat inflammatory bowel conditions.

Like other fermented foods (tea, coffee, yogurt, sourdough bread, sauerkraut), this drink provides food in the form of sugar for the wild microorganisms floating around and on us at all times. In return, those tiny organisms multiply and replenish the microorganisms that live in our insides, helping to keep us well.

Makes about 2 cups

> 2 large pieces (each 2-inches long) fresh ginger root, divided
> 1/2 cup sugar, divided
> 2 cups cold, non-chlorinated water

Wash your hands and start with clean utensils and a quart glass jar. There is no need to sterilize since the culture comes from bacteria on you, in the air, and in your kitchen.

Peel (if the ginger is not organic) and grate 1 piece of ginger into the quart jar. Add 3 tablespoons of sugar and the water. Stir with a wooden spoon. Cover the jar with a piece of cheesecloth or a paper coffee filter secured with a rubber band. Set aside on your countertop (do not refrigerate).

Every day for the next 5 days, stir the mixture and add 1 table-spoon grated ginger and 1 tablespoon sugar. The mixture will start to ferment—bubbles form at the top and the mixture smells slightly sweet and yeasty—usually within 5 days, but it could take as long as 7 to 8 days of adding grated ginger and sugar to start the fermentation. Mould should not appear, but if it does, scrape it off and if it reoccurs, start the process again.

When you see signs of fermentation (described in step 3 above), refrigerate.

To use the lightly carbonated, ginger drink, strain the liquid using a fine mesh strainer. Save the grated ginger in a sealed container and use in recipes calling for fresh ginger or compost it. Store the strained ginger liquid in a clean jar with a lid for up to 3 weeks, adding 1 teaspoon each of grated ginger and sugar once per week.

To Use Ginger Bug for Fizzy Drinks: In a jug, combine 1/4 cup strained Ginger Bug and 4 cups mint or lemon herbal tea or fresh apple, peach, pear, or orange juice.

Ginger Tepache

Tepache is a Mexican-style, fresh water or "agua fresca" beverage that is similar to Ginger Bug, but fermented by the sun, which speeds up the fermentation process. Like Sun Tea or Moon Water, this cool and refreshing drink is set outside, in the garden to take warmth and energy from the sun. This recipe uses the peel from a whole pineapple, making it a Reduce Food Waste recipe. Brown sugar can be used instead of piloncillo.

Makes about 2 cups

> 4 cups water
> Juice of 1/2 lemon
> 1/2 cup piloncillo (unrefined, pure cane sugar)
> 1 fresh pineapple
> 1 2-inch piece ginger root, chopped
> 1 2-inch stick cinnamon
> Fruited Ginger Syrup to taste (recipe follows) or maple syrup

Combine water, lemon juice, and sugar in a large saucepan. Bring to a boil over high heat and stir until sugar is dissolved. Remove pan from the heat.

Wash the pineapple, cut the top off and discard it. Cut away the outside peel and cut it into chunks. Add peel to the water mixture in the pan. Remove the hard core from the pineapple, coarsely chop, and add it to the pan. Tightly cover the pineapple flesh and refrigerate for another use or use it to garnish tepache drinks.

Stir in ginger and cinnamon. Cover the pan with a kitchen towel and set it outside, on a table or chair, in the sun.

Check for fermentation after 24 to 36 hours. Some frothy white foam on the surface of the water means that the mixture is fermenting. You can strain off the tepache, chill, and drink once you see fermentation or let it continue to ferment for another

24 hours if you want more carbonation. The longer the liquid ferments, the stronger the taste and the amount of alcohol produced.

Before serving, taste the chilled drink and add more water and/ or some syrup as desired. Add chopped fresh pineapple, orange slices, or cherries as a garnish.

Fruited Ginger Syrup

Used to sweeten and enhance cocktails, iced juices, teas, refreshers, and smoothies, this syrup is versatile because it complements so many flavours. For a lighter fruit flavour, use perfectly ripe pears or peaches in place of the apples.

Makes 1 cup

> 1 cup water
> 1 cup granulated sugar
> 2 cups coarsely chopped apples, skin on
> 2-inch piece fresh ginger, peeled and chopped or grated
> 2 tablespoons grated orange or lemon zest
> 1 tablespoon apple cider vinegar

Bring the water to a boil in a saucepan over high heat. Stir in sugar and stir until dissolved. Add apples, ginger, zest, and vinegar. Reduce heat and keep the mixture simmering for 30 minutes. Remove from heat and set aside to cool.

Strain syrup through a fine-mesh strainer, pressing on the solids to extract as much flavour as possible. Compost solids and pour liquid into a clean glass jar with lid. Label and refrigerate for up to 2 weeks.

Zingi-Fresca

It's Agua Fresca, or "cool water" with a definite spike of ginger and it's the ideal drink any season, any time of day because it hydrates and nourishes the very cells of our bodies. This is a healthy ritual to add to your daily H_2O intake. Any fresh soft, fleshy berries or stone fruit—cherries, plums, peaches, apricots—will work.

Makes 3 cups

> 1/2 lemon
> 2 cups water
> 1 cup coarsely chopped pineapple
> 1 cup coarsely chopped honeydew melon or stone fruit
> 1-inch piece fresh ginger, chopped
> Fruited Ginger Syrup or honey to taste

Peel away the zest and white pith from the lemon. Remove seeds and coarsely chop the flesh into the jug of a blender. Add the water, pineapple, melon, and ginger and blend on high for about 2 minutes or until smooth.

Taste and add a tablespoon of syrup or honey, as desired.

Iced Ginger "Ade"

Even with the ginger and chile pepper, in a weirdly wonderful way, this chiller with heat works to slake thirst in the dense heat of summer. You could make it a Shandy by adding non- or alcoholic Ginger Beer. Try carrot juice or lemon-ginger tea in place of the Ginger Bug.

> 1 cup Ginger Bug or Tepache or water
> 4 ice cubes

2 cups cubed cantaloupe melon, pineapple, or mango
3 tablespoons Fruited Ginger Syrup or maple syrup or honey
Juice of 1/2 lemon or lime
1 1/2-inch piece ginger, peeled and sliced
1/2 small jalapeño pepper, trimmed and sliced

Combine Ginger Bug, ice, cantaloupe, syrup, lemon juice, ginger, and pepper in a blender jug. Blend on 'high' for 2 minutes or until smooth.

Gingered Chocolate Smoothie

This one is a keeper. Easy to make anytime, it's especially useful at breakfast because it brings nut protein to your hungry tummy. And the fibre in the fruit has enough staying power to fuel your morning. Make it the night before for a quick getaway (shake, sip, and sigh with pleasure).

Makes 2 drinks

1 1/2 cups almond milk
1 banana, fresh or frozen, peeled and cut into chunks
6 dates, chopped
3 tablespoons peanut butter (smooth or crunchy)
3 tablespoons cocoa powder
2 tablespoons hemp hearts
2 tablespoons chia seeds
1 tablespoon chopped fresh or candied ginger

Combine almond milk, banana, dates, peanut butter, cocoa powder, hemp hearts, chia seeds, and ginger in a blender jug. Blend on 'high' for 2 minutes or until smooth.

Footnotes

1 *A History of Herbal Plants*, Richard Le Strange; page 262.

2 as above

References

Le Strange, Richard. *A History of Herbal Plants*. New York: Arco Publishing Company Inc., 1977.

The Serious Eats Team. "11 Ginger Drinks to Make at Home." 8-9-2018. https://www.seriouseats.com/ginger-drinks-cocktail-recipes-fall-drinks-with-fresh-ginger-canton-liqueur. Accessed 2-1-2023.

Hackett, Jolinda. "Ginger Root Tea." 6-30-2022. https://www.thespruceeats.com/homemade-ginger-tea-3377239. Accessed 2-1-2023

Pat Crocker's mission in life is to write with insight and experience, cook with playful abandon, and eat herbs with gusto. As a professional Home Economist (BAA, Toronto Metropolitan University) and Culinary Herbalist, Pat's passion for healthy food is fused with her knowledge and love of herbs. She has honed her wellness practice over more than four decades of growing, photographing, and writing about what she calls, the helping plants. In fact, Crocker infuses the medicinal benefits of herbs in every original recipe she develops.

An award-winning author, Pat received the G.H. Foster Award for Excellence in Herbal Literature and has written 23 herb/healthy cookbooks, including *The Herbalist's Kitchen* (Sterling, 2018), *The Healing Herbs Cookbook*, and *The Juicing Bible*.

www.patcrocker.com; Instagram: @pc1writes

PICKLED-GINGER-BACK COCKTAIL

Karen England

The secret to making great cocktails in general and a ginger cocktail specifically is in no small part due to using quality ingredients, because a bad spirit or mixer will make a bad cocktail. Quality ingredients are not necessarily expensive (and vice versa.) The most expensive spirits out there don't make cocktails any better, so if you are lucky enough to own a pricey booze of any kind, save it for sipping straight (without anything added). Making your own cocktail ingredients not only saves money but means that your final products can be organic, should you use organic ingredients; tailored to your own taste, homegrown, avoiding allergens, preservatives, unnatural colorants and other undesirable things often found in commercial products.

Pickled-Ginger-Back

While in New York in 2015, I discovered a cocktail called the "Pickleback." Maybe you've heard of it? I learned of it while I was on a vacation pub crawl with family and friends in the Red Hook section of Brooklyn, New York.

Supposedly the drink, which consists of a shot of Jameson Whiskey chased with a shot of pickle brine, was invented in 2006, largely because it was thought that drinking pickle brine might ward off a hangover. The drink quickly rocketed and became a worldwide sensation. I have loved the drink ever since I first tasted it and have made several variants over the years utilizing brine from my homemade pickles, pickled eggs, zucchini pickles, chard stem pickles and pickled ginger.

My most legendary version so far of the Pickleback cocktail involved my pickled eggs and led to this, my latest Pickleback variation, inspired by my addiction to sushi.

Serves one

   1 plump cucumber for making the edible shot glasses, optional
   1.5 ounces Japanese Whisky (such as Suntory), well chilled
   1.5 ounces sushi pickled ginger, well-chilled
   Ground pink peppercorns, for garnish

To make cucumber shot glasses, peel the cucumber if desired, trim the ends and cut into two large logs. Partially hollow out logs, leaving both with solid bottoms, forming two edible shot glasses.

Fill one cucumber shot with whisky and the other with pickled ginger brine. Season both with ground pink peppercorns and serve immediately.

First drink the whisky, then drink the brine. Finally, eat the cucumber shot glasses.

Pickled-Ginger-Back cocktails are fun served in edible cucumber shot glasses.
Karen England

Karen's favorite pickled ginger recipe is "Ming Tsai's Pickled Ginger", and the recipe can be found at https://www.foodnetwork.com/recipes/pickled-ginger-recipe-1949982.

A tip from Ming: "Though pickled ginger will turn a nice pink color over time, I often use beets or red shiso leaves to tint the pickle delicately. Though hard to come by, the red shiso provides superior color and an herby flavor."

Or see Susan Belsinger's recipe for "Pungent Pickled Ginger", in this book.

References

Tsai, Ming and Boehm, Arthur, C. *Blue Ginger: East meets West cooking with Ming Tsai.* New York: Clarkson Potter, 1999.

Karen England *lives, works and gardens on two steeply sloping acres in Vista, a small town in northern San Diego County, California, just nine miles as a crow flies from the Pacific Ocean. When she's not drinking herbal cocktails, she drinks tea. Find her on Instagram @edgehillherbfarm. Listen to "Herbs Make The Difference" Podcast, a new podcast from Karen and edgehillherbfarm.blog that can be found on Apple Podcasts, Spotify, Amazon Music, and more.*

Pickled ginger with shiso leaf
Susan Belsinger

This very fresh form of just-harvested ginger, although pungent, is not quite as hot as cured, brown-skinned ginger. It is a real treat--crisp, yet much more tender with less inner fiber, and the bright flavor is superb.

Susan Belsinger

GINGER ~ THE UNDERGROUND FLAVOR

Donna Frawley

The first written record of ginger was in China, stating that Confucius ate ginger with every meal. In 406 AD, a monk wrote that ginger was grown in pots and carried on Chinese ships to prevent scurvy. Ginger was introduced to the Mediterranean by the Arabs. In 150 AD, it was noted that ginger was produced in Ceylon. Raw and preserved ginger was imported into Europe during the Middle Ages where it was described in the official pharmacopeias of several countries. In 14th century England, a pound of ginger cost as much as a sheep.

If you don't want to grow your own ginger, in the grocery store it comes in five forms: fresh rhizomes; paste (ground fresh ginger in a tube); fresh, sliced thin and pickled; dried and then ground; and crystallized (fresh, sliced and cooked in a sugar syrup). Fresh ginger can also be frozen. It is best to cut the fresh rhizome into recipe-size servings and then put it in a freezer bag or container, label and date. It keeps in the freezer for about six months. When you are ready to use it you don't even need to thaw it out, because frozen ginger peels and grates more easily when it is frozen. Peel ginger with a spoon instead of a vegetable peeler; this does a better job and is safer for your fingers. If you are slicing it, however, peel first and then thaw before slicing.

Ginger is not used exclusively in Asian cuisine, but along with garlic it is considered a staple in the Asian kitchen. It is included in light sauces and to flavor stir-fry oils. Ginger is used for both flavor and its curative powers.

Japanese Restaurant-Style Salad Dressing with Mixed Greens

Serves 4

> 1/2 cup minced onion
> 1/2 cup peanut oil
> 1/3 cup rice wine vinegar
> 2 tablespoons water
> 2 tablespoons minced fresh ginger root
> 2 tablespoons minced celery
> 2 tablespoons ketchup
> 4 teaspoons soy sauce
> 2 teaspoons white sugar
> 2 teaspoons lemon juice
> 1/2 teaspoon minced garlic
> 1/2 teaspoon salt
> 1/4 teaspoon ground black pepper
> 8 cups mixed spring salad greens
> 1/2 cup shredded carrots
> 1/2 cup parsley, minced

In a blender, combine the minced onion, peanut oil, rice wine vinegar, water, ginger, celery, ketchup, soy sauce, sugar, lemon juice, garlic, salt and pepper. Blend on high speed for about 30 seconds or until all the ingredients are puréed.

In a large bowl, mix greens, carrots, and parsley. Place in individual bowls and drizzle on dressing.

Mango Ginger Rice

Serves 4 to 6

- 2 tablespoons canola oil
- 1/4 cup chopped dried mango or other dried fruit
- 2 teaspoons minced fresh ginger root
- 1 cup uncooked jasmine rice
- 2 cups water
- 1/2 teaspoon salt
- 1/4 cup chopped green onions
- 1 tablespoon chopped fresh tarragon
- 2 tablespoons chopped fresh cilantro, optional

Heat oil in a saucepan over medium-low heat. Sauté mango and ginger until fragrant, 2 to 3 minutes. Add rice and sauté, stirring often, until rice appears translucent, about 5 minutes. Pour in water and salt; bring to a boil. Reduce heat and cover; cook until water is absorbed, about 20 minutes.

Transfer hot rice to a serving dish and top with green onions, tarragon and cilantro. Serve with pork chops or chicken filets.

Marinated Pork with Ginger-Apple Compote

Serves 4

Marinade for pork

  2 cups balsamic vinegar
  2 tablespoons minced garlic
  1 tablespoon chopped fresh thyme
  1 teaspoon chopped fresh rosemary
  1 cup olive oil
  1 pork tenderloin (about 1 pound), or 4 1-inch pork tenderloin chops

Compote

  1/2 cup butter
  1/4 cup brown sugar
  1 apple, thinly sliced
  1/4 cup dried cherries or craisins
  1 tablespoon minced fresh ginger root
  1 pinch ground cinnamon
  1 pinch ground nutmeg

To make the marinade, purée the balsamic vinegar, garlic, thyme, and rosemary in a blender until mixed. With the blender running, slowly pour in the olive oil until thickened and incorporated.

Pour the marinade into a resealable plastic bag. Add the pork pieces, coat with the marinade, squeeze out excess air, and seal the bag. Marinate in the refrigerator for 30 minutes.

Preheat an outdoor grill for medium heat, and lightly oil the grate. Remove the pork from the marinade and shake off excess. Discard the remaining marinade.

Cook the pork on the preheated grill until no longer pink in the center, about 10 minutes.

Or, to cook the pork under the broiler in your oven, preheat broiler. Adjust rack to 6 inches away from broiler. Put meat on a broiler pan and set under broiler for 5 minutes then turn over and broil 4 to 5 minutes longer. An instant-read thermometer inserted into the center should read 145°F.

Once cooked, remove from heat, cover with aluminum foil, and allow to rest for 5 to 10 minutes. Slice the tenderloin pieces.

Prepare the compote while the pork is cooking. Melt the butter in a saucepan over medium heat and stir in the brown sugar until it begins to simmer. Add the apples, cherries or craisins, ginger, cinnamon, and nutmeg. Cook and stir until the apple is tender, about 5 minutes. Serve the sliced pork topped with the apple compote.

Ginger Sticks

This is a nice breakfast bread, served with coffee or tea. If you do not have pearl sugar, raw sugar can be substituted.

Makes 48 sticks or rolls

2 packages active dry yeast
2/3 cup warm water (105 to 115°F)
1 cup warm milk (105 to 115°F)

1/2 cup sugar
1 1/2 teaspoons salt
1/4 cup soft butter
2 eggs
5 to 6 cups flour
1/4 cup finely chopped crystallized ginger
1 teaspoon ground cinnamon
Cooking oil
1 egg white, lightly beaten
6 tablespoons pearl or raw sugar

In a large bowl sprinkle in yeast and pour in water. Stir until yeast is dissolved. Add warm milk, sugar, salt, butter, eggs and 3 cups flour. Beat with electric mixer on low speed until smooth, about 1 minute. Add ginger and cinnamon, turn up beater to medium, and beat for 2 to 3 minutes until thick and elastic. Scrape sides of bowl occasionally.

Stir in remaining flour gradually with a wooden spoon. Use just enough flour to make a soft dough which leaves the sides of the bowl. Turn out onto a floured board (adding more flour if needed) and knead for 5 to 10 minutes until dough is smooth and elastic. Cover and let the dough rest on the board for 20 minutes.

Punch down. Divide dough into two equal parts. With a rolling pin, roll each part into a 9 x 12-inch rectangle on a lightly greased board. Cut the long side into twelve 1-inch strips. Cut each strip in half crosswise. Twist each strip and place close together in 2 greased 9 x 13-inch pans. Brush surface of dough with oil. Cover pans loosely with plastic wrap. Refrigerate for 2 to 24 hours.

When ready to bake, remove from refrigerator, uncover and let stand on counter 20 minutes while you preheat the oven to 375°F. Brush with beaten egg white and sprinkle with pearl or raw sugar just before baking. Bake on the lower oven rack for 20 to 25 minutes or until done. Remove from pans and cool on wire racks.

Donna Frawley *has owned and run Frawley's Fine Herbary for 40 years and has developed 60 culinary herb blends, 8 herb flavored vinegars, and 8 herbal teas. Her passions include gardening, cooking and baking, particularly with herbs, and most of all sharing what she has learned in life with others.*

Donna loves to share and write about all her passions. She is the author of monthly articles for two publications, her own weekly newsletter, and The Herbal Breads Cookbook and Our Favorite Recipes, available on her website: frawleysfineherbary.com.

She has written a new book called 100 Ways to Make a Difference: Creating Ripples of Love for a Lasting Legacy.

GINGERLICIOUS

Cooper Murray

I started eating ginger in early childhood not knowing how much I would love the herb many years later. My grandmother grew ginger in her beautiful garden and dried it to use throughout the winter. When my brother Ernie was visiting, I shared with him my thoughts on ginger recipes I had in mind. His quick response was, "You will be including Zazvornicky." Funny how growing up with ginger seems to linger with us. And yes, Zazvornicky is included in my favorites I have shared.

Ginger has so many different qualities and amazing benefits. Whether it is added to recipes fresh, pickled as a condiment or taken medicinally, it is truly a gift from God. Ginger is always there, whether in the forefront or in the shadows. I can't imagine my kitchen without this old funny- looking herb we so love.

Asian Chicken and Ginger Soup

Our family loves a good bowl of nourishing soup. We enjoy soup year-round, and this Asian Chicken and Ginger Soup is one of our favorites. I like to serve the rice on the side for a low carb alternative. If you're wanting added protein, substitute bone broth for the chicken broth. Don't wait until you feel under the weather to make this soup.

Serves 5

    1 tablespoon olive oil
    1 tablespoon sesame oil
    2 garlic cloves, minced
    3-inch fresh ginger root, peeled and sliced into matchsticks
    1/2 cup carrots, sliced
    1 cup white mushrooms, sliced
    5 bone-in, skinless chicken thighs
    1 tablespoon soy sauce
    1 tablespoons rice wine vinegar
    6 cups low-sodium chicken broth
    3 green onions, sliced
    1 cup jasmine rice, cooked

Heat the olive and sesame oil in a soup pan or Dutch oven over medium heat. Add the garlic, ginger, carrots and mushrooms. Stir and sauté for 3 minutes.

Add the chicken thighs. Top with soy sauce, rice wine vinegar and chicken broth. Stir to mix ingredients. Bring to a boil, then lower heat to a simmer. Simmer for 1 hour.

Ginger adds extra flavor and healing qualities to soup.

Remove chicken from the pot. Remove all bones and shred the chicken. Return to the pot with the green onions. Serve in soup bowls with rice on the side.

Mini Penne Pasta with Ginger and Basil

I originally found this recipe in an old cookbook by French Chef Pierre Franey; it is available online now at https://nytimes.com. It caught my attention because ginger is not usually added to a pasta dish unless it is Asian in origin. The ginger and basil combination really complimented each other. This is a simple, comforting dish that can be made in 20 minutes. I have adapted the recipe slightly to suit my cooking style and likings. A microplane zester is the best tool for grated ginger. Great as a vegetarian entrée or side dish.

Serves 4

- 2 tablespoons salt
- 1/2 pound mini penne pasta
- 4 tablespoons butter
- 2 tablespoons olive oil
- 2 tablespoons fresh ginger, grated
- 3 green onions, thinly sliced
- 2 teaspoons fresh garlic, minced
- 1/2 cup Parmesan cheese, grated
- 1/2 teaspoon salt
- 1/2 teaspoon pepper
- 1/2 cup fresh basil leaves, torn into medium pieces

Add 2 tablespoons salt to a large pot of water. Bring to a boil. Add mini penne pasta. Stir, bring to a boil again, stirring often.

Cook 10 minutes for al dente pasta. Drain and reserve 1/2 cup of cooking liquid.

In a large sauté pan, melt the butter and add the olive oil. Add the ginger, green onions and garlic. Cook for 3 minutes until softened. Add the pasta and reserved cooking liquid, stirring well to blend. Add the Parmesan cheese, salt, pepper, and basil. Toss well and serve.

Zazvornicky ~ Slovak Ginger Cookies

Each Christmas I would help my grandmother make these little treasure cookies for the holiday season using special Zazvornicky cookie cutters. It was not until much later; I learned the shape of the Zazvornicky cookie cutter actually resembled the shape of a ginger root. I am sharing my grandmother's recipe. These light crisp cookies are wonderful for a snack served with tea. They are well worth the time it takes to make them.

Makes 24 cookies

8 egg yolks
1 pound powdered sugar
4 egg whites, beaten stiff
1/2 cup butter, melted
2 teaspoons baking powder
2 teaspoons ground ginger
4 cups flour, sifted
Non-stick cooking spray

Ginger root-shaped cookie cutter.

Using a stand mixer or hand-held mixer, mix egg yolks with confectioner's sugar, beating well for 10 minutes. Add egg whites, melted butter, baking powder and ginger.

Add flour gradually, beating on medium until mixed. Put on a lightly floured board and refrigerate 30 minutes. The less the dough is handled, the better.

Divide the dough in half to roll out one at a time. Roll about 1/4 to 1/2-inch thick and cut out cookies. Place on lightly greased cookie sheet. Let stand overnight until dry. Do not cover.

Preheat oven to 400°F. Brush off flour from the tops of the cookies before baking. Bake for 5 to 6 minutes or until lightly tan in color on top and baked on the bottom. Store in a sealed container.

Cooper's recommendation for making Ginger Honey No-Churn Ice Cream:

I cannot say enough good things about this ice cream! I have never owned an ice cream maker; they seem like a lot of work. Based on the recipe "Turmeric Ginger No-Churn Ice Cream" from Loreto and Nicoletta, Sugar Love Spices Blog, I omitted the turmeric and increased the ginger. Ginger is one of my favorite herbs, especially in desserts. This ice cream tastes amazingly creamy; you will be delighted with the results.

Ginger Honey No-Churn Ice Cream.

References
Franey, Pierre. "Penne Pasta with Ginger and Basil." https://nytimes.com. Accessed 2-22-23.

Loreto and Nicoletta, "Turmeric Ginger No-Churn Ice Cream." https://www.sugarlovesspices.com. Accessed 6/2020.

Photos by Cooper Murray.

Tamara "Cooper" Murray, *BA, MA is a graduate of Nazareth College and the University of Kansas. Originally from Binghamton, New York, and living for many years in Colorado, she now calls Alabama her home. Cooper's influence came from her grandmother Vilma who immigrated to the United States and became a private cook in New York City. Cooper furthered her culinary knowledge working at country clubs and restaurants. She creates recipes that highlight herbs and has written for numerous magazines and publications. Cooper's fondness for herbs and cooking led her to develop Organic Herbal Cooking, Inc., which offers motivational and educational cooking events in the southeast. Cooper is also Special Events Director at Burritt on the Mountain, a living history museum in Huntsville, Alabama. She loves herbs and usually any conversation with her leads to talking about fresh herbs! Not a day goes by that Cooper is not savoring the benefits of cooking with herbs.*

Grated ginger is a great start for any recipe--brown sugar
and molasses go well with ginger's pungency.
Janice Cox

GINGER MEMORIES

Diann Nance

Ginger was always a special herb in my home as I was growing up. My mother used ginger in crisp desserts, not soft gingerbread. However, when I was in high school, gingerbread became "humble pie" for me. We had a math teacher who did not have good class control and became a victim of our sophomore practical jokes. One day he brought delicious gingerbread for us. It made me grow up a little and realize how mean we had been. To this day as I enjoy making and eating gingerbread, I think of that teacher and how he used ginger to teach me more than math.

Enjoy this very moist, spicy gingerbread with butter or cream cheese. Keep for a couple of days before slicing.

Spicy Ginger Gingerbread

Yields 8 slices
  1 1/2 cups all-purpose flour
  1/2 teaspoon salt
  1 tablespoon ground ginger
  1 1/2 teaspoons ground cinnamon
  1/4 teaspoon grated nutmeg

1/8 teaspoon ground allspice

1 tablespoon flour

1/3 grated candied ginger

1/2 cup dark molasses

1/2 cup golden syrup

1/2 cup packed light brown sugar

1 cup milk

1/2 cup unsalted butter, chilled and diced

1 extra-large egg, beaten

Spicy Ginger Gingerbread is good with cream cheese.
Diann Nance

Preheat the oven to 350°F. Grease a 9 x 5 x 3-inch loaf pan and line the bottom with parchment.

Sift the flour, baking powder, baking soda, salt and all spices into a large mixing bowl.

In a small bowl, mix 1 tablespoon flour with grated candied ginger and reserve.

In a small saucepan melt the molasses with the golden syrup, then let cool to lukewarm. In a small bowl, dissolve the sugar in the milk in the microwave, stirring occasionally.

Add the diced butter to the flour mixture and rub in with your fingertips (or use a food processor) until the mixture resembles fine crumbs. Add the floured candied ginger to the flour mixture.

Whisk the milk mixture into the flour mixture, then whisk in the molasses mixture, followed by the beaten egg. When thoroughly blended, you should have a thin batter.

Pour the batter into the prepared pan and bake for 45 minutes to one hour or until a skewer inserted into the center comes out clean. The gingerbread will rise during baking then shrink slightly as it cools. Allow to cool completely in the pan. Turn out and wrap first in parchment paper and then in foil to keep fresh for a few days.

Diann Nance, born and raised on a farm in north central Texas, is presently living and growing herbs among the beautiful rolling hills of north central Tennessee. After a forty-year teaching career which included time spent in Texas, Taiwan, Germany, and finally Tennessee, she realized a long-held dream of starting a plant-growing business. Although Diann is now retired from the business of herbs, she still grows and uses herbs on a regular basis. Her interest in herbs and their uses in our daily lives can be attributed to her mother and grandmother, who loved plants and sharing their knowledge of herbs and plants in general.

Diann continues this tradition by growing plants, conducting workshops, and demonstrating the uses of herbs. She is a Master Gardener, a member of the Beachaven Garden Club, The Herb Society of America, and The International Herb Association. She a lifelong learner and may be contacted at dinance40@gmail.com

MY GINGER HARVEST

Marge Powell

I garden in Northeast Florida, zone 9a, and ginger is a perennial plant here. About four years ago I planted pieces of sprouted ginger in my garden. I had purchased the ginger from my local supermarket, and I can only assume it was *Zingiber officinale*. This is difficult to authenticate because I suspect even the store's produce buyers are unaware of the actual cultivar. When this ginger bloomed, I thought that I could use the bloom to validate the species. This plant blooms in a terminal spike with many individual flowers. That was not as helpful as I expected; because there is so much misinformation on ginger blooms, I could not find a definitive image. So, I have settled on this: I bought it from the grocery store, I liked the taste, it sprouted, I planted it, it grew, and now it was long past time to harvest it. And I will call it "edible ginger."

The ginger dies back in the winter and reemerges about February. Now it is fall. It has had a full eight months of maturity this growing season. The flower spikes have dried, and the leaves have yellowed, so it is time to get out the shovel and dig the ginger rhizomes. This is not an easy task. Over the years the plants have multiplied, and the roots are a tangled mass. If you are growing ginger in a pot, your harvest will be much easier. I cut down the stalks to make digging easier.

**Ginger rhizomes with several years'
root growth.**

At last, the clump is free of the garden. This looks like a large clump, but it is less than 25% of my stand of edible ginger. The first problem is to get as much soil away from the clump as possible. I used a garden hose but found myself wishing I had a pressure washer.

I relocated to my deck where I could work with the clump of rhizomes (with roots still attached) on a table. After the initial wash to remove the garden soil, I used heavy duty clippers to start to cut the clumps apart. This was necessary to continue to remove the soil from the clump. When I had separated the clump into individual sections, I was able to do a more thorough job of soil removal.

After most of the soil was cleaned away, I used my garden shears to remove the tops and roots. As each piece was trimmed, I dropped it into a bowl of water, which helped to rid the rhizomes of any remaining soil. I changed the water in the bowl three times.

Trimmed rhizomes were washed mutiple times.

I thought the soil removal was going to be the hardest part of this job; instead, it was scraping the "skin" and rhizome stubs to get a clean piece of ginger. I suspect ignoring harvesting the ginger for years allowed the roots to grow thick as they emerged from the rhizome. This has resulted in a new garden resolution: move the edible ginger to its own plot and harvest annually.

It was time to move to the kitchen. I weighed my rhizomes–20 ounces. My goal was to make ginger paste and ginger-garlic paste. Many recipes say to cube the ginger and then process it into a paste in the food processor. I preferred to use the food processor to first slice all the ginger harvest, rather than cube it. I divided the sliced ginger into two batches of about 10 ounces each.

**Processed and cleaned rhizomes--ready
to make ginger pastes.**

Ginger Paste

To make the ginger paste, I put 10 ounces of sliced ginger into the food processor with the major blade. I added approximately 1/3 cup of olive oil as the ginger was processing. This was to add moisture to the ginger and take advantage of the oil acting as a preservative. As the ginger processed (and this took a few minutes), I would stop the processor and check the moisture level of the paste. I did not want it dry, but I also did not want it "soupy."

Ginger-Garlic Paste

The ginger-garlic paste is more complex. I will use it in stir fries or other savory dishes where a ginger-garlic combination is appropriate. I put the last 10 ounces of sliced ginger into the food processor and added the peeled cloves of an entire head of garlic. I also added 1 tablespoon of dried ground turmeric and about 2 tablespoons of tamari. I used between 1/3 and 1/2 cup of olive oil to keep the mixture moist, but not runny. Both the oil and the turmeric act as preservatives. I processed this to the consistency of a paste, checking as it went along to see if more olive oil was needed.

I put each paste into an ice cube tray. Once they are frozen, the cubes will go into labeled plastic bags and be kept in the freezer. When I want to add the zing of ginger, I will retrieve one of the ginger paste cubes for use in the dish I am making.

The ginger taste is not as strong as I would like; but with time the taste may develop. The ginger zing is certainly there. This whole process took me about three hours, and it was time well spent. I will really appreciate this when instead of peeling and grating ginger and garlic, all I must do is drop a frozen cube or two into my recipe.

Ginger Paste and Ginger-Garlic Paste.

Photos by Marge Powell.

"A piece of ginger candy is a great pick-me-up when you are dragging in the afternoon." ---Skye Suter

Susan Belsinger

GINGER IS MY FAVORITE HERB

Skye Suter

Ginger is my favorite herb– well, one of them. I cherish so many herbs that my favorite often tends to be the one directly confronting me. But ginger has held a special place for me since I was a small child.

Ginger has many positive attributes in both its medicinal and culinary forms. Eating ginger in food preparations often covers both bases. Sushi and sashimi are always served with "sushi ginger" which is pickled ginger. The ginger acts as a palate cleanser and is eaten in-between the bite-sized offerings, or at the same time. Ginger (and wasabi, which is also served with sushi) help to aid digestion and kill bacteria that might be encountered while eating raw fish.

Chewy ginger candy also serves this dual purpose. I keep some in the car because it is incredibly helpful for motion sickness or stomach upset from an unsatisfactory meal out. I also keep it in the house as a candy snack. A piece of ginger candy is a great pick-me-up when you are dragging in the afternoon.

I enjoy consuming ginger in many ways, whether alone or added to some yummy dish. Ginger's appeal goes back to childhood memories of Christmas, when my brother and I received an annual bag of candied ginger. I recently asked my mother why she gave us ginger only at Christmas. She said it was the only time of year when candied ginger was available. Nowadays it can be purchased at any time of year.

Ginger is a common ingredient in cuisine from all over the world, especially in Asian and Middle Eastern cuisines. Many an Indian curry or Thai soup have gotten heat from a knob or two of ginger. The famous and very delicious Indian chai is made from black tea with spices including ginger, and sometimes milk. Most Chinese food dishes also have ginger. As a child living in a foreign nation (India) with spicy culinary traditions, I often ate ginger, whether it was served to me in a curry, vegetable dish, or sweet confection, deepening my love for ginger.

Recipes from previous centuries often called for ginger. We find ginger in our grandmother's recipe boxes as well as in colonial American "receipts". Romans and other ancient cultures, and Medieval Europeans, used ginger extensively. The famous Scarborough Faire had numerous stalls selling breads, cookies and other goodies made with ginger. To this day, I love candied ginger and all forms of Indian food. But I also like gingersnaps more than I ought, and gingerbread, and holiday gingerbread men and women, and the steamed carrot cake my grandma used to make.

We add ginger to our recipes in different forms – dried, preserved, and fresh. Dried ginger comes in powdered form and also in small, dried pieces. Candied ginger is used in recipes as an ingredient, and on top as a flavorful garnish. A "knob" of ginger is a piece of the rhizome, usually about an inch long, which is added to flavor a recipe, and is not meant to be eaten. Fresh ginger is also sliced into "coins" or grated into a recipe.

Ginger root from the grocery will generally have a papery skin. In most instances this skin is peeled away before grating or cutting into pieces. Softer skin on ginger will easily peel with the side of a spoon, while older ginger may require the use of a paring knife.

When selecting ginger at the market look for firm, plump pieces with light, even-toned skins. Avoid rhizomes which are dried out and wrinkly or look like they are starting to sprout.

Here is an assortment of recipes with ginger from my grand-mother's recipe book. I enjoyed many of them when she baked them, and I have also made them when feeling nostalgic as an adult. They are all delicious and worth a little time in the kitchen.

Grandma's Chopped Apple Cake

Apples and ginger are two ingredients that make me think of baking and my grandmother Myrtle. The ingredients in her recipes are common to all baking lists; ginger and spices, plus flour, sugar, salt, eggs, and leavening, combine here to create something memorably delicious. This recipe could have been baked by any grandmother to be eaten with delight by her grandchildren.

Serves 9 to 12

   2 cups flour
   1/2 teaspoon salt
   1 teaspoon soda
   1 teaspoon ground cinnamon
   1/2 teaspoon ground ginger
   1 cup sugar
   2 eggs
   1 cup oil
   1 teaspoon vanilla
   3 cups chopped apple
   1/2 cup chopped nuts

Sift together the flour, salt, soda, cinnamon, ginger, and sugar. Add the oil, eggs and vanilla. Beat well. Add chopped apples and nuts.

Place batter in greased 9 x 12-inch cake pan or large loaf pan.

Bake 1 hour at 350ºF. Serve warm or cold.

Grandma Myrtle's Steamed Carrot Pudding with Lemon Sauce

I was really crazy for this carrot pudding (which was more like a cake) and was thrilled every time Grandma made it. As an adult, I was reluctant to make it because of the carrot grating involved but was always glad that I did when it came time to eat it.

Grandma always used her canner as a steamer, but any large pot will do if your cake pan will fit in the steamer. If not using a steamer, you will need to set up some type of rack in the bottom to keep the cake pan from sitting in water. Serve with lemon sauce; recipe follows.

Serves 12

Carrot Pudding

- 1 cup shortening
- 1 cup brown sugar
- 2 eggs, slightly beaten
- 3 cups raw carrots, grated
- 1 cup currants (can substitute raisins)
- 1 cup raisins
- 2 1/2 cups all-purpose flour
- 4 teaspoons baking powder
- 1 teaspoon salt
- 1 teaspoon ground cinnamon
- 1 teaspoon ground ginger
- 1 teaspoon ground nutmeg
- 2 tablespoons water, as needed

In a large bowl, combine the shortening, brown sugar and eggs. Add the grated carrots, currants and raisins.

In a separate bowl combine and whisk the flour, baking powder, salt, cinnamon, ginger, and nutmeg.

Add about 1/3 of the dry ingredients to the wet and mix. Repeat until everything is combined. Add up to 2 tablespoons of water if mix is too dry. The carrot pudding will get plenty of moisture while it is steaming. Scrape and pour the mixture into an angel food cake pan.

Set up a canning steamer with the rack at the bottom and pour water to a level below where the cake pan will sit. Place the pan of pudding into a canning steamer on the rack and steam for 1 1/2 to 2 hours. Check occasionally and add some water if needed. Place it in a low temperature oven (about 300ºF) for 10 minutes if needed to reduce sogginess.

Lemon Sauce

2 cups water

1 cup sugar

Juice and zest of 1 lemon

2 tablespoons cornstarch

1 to 2 tablespoons butter

Place water, sugar, lemon juice and zest, and cornstarch in a saucepan and cook, stirring constantly, until the sugar dissolves and the cornstarch thickens it into a sauce consistency. Stir in the butter.

Serve warm sauce over a piece of the carrot pudding. It's the best!

Molasses Cookies

Molasses cookies are a real old-fashioned favorite that you don't see around much these days. Next time you feel the need for a comforting, homey cookie, try making some molasses cookies. My grandmother's cookbook had multiple recipes for similar cookies. This recipe is attributed to Genie Clement, who was one of grandma's relatives.

Makes 3 to 4 dozen

1 cup shortening

1 cup sugar

1 cup molasses

4 level teaspoons baking soda

2 teaspoons ground ginger

2 teaspoons ground cinnamon
1/2 teaspoon ground cloves
1/4 teaspoon ground nutmeg
1 teaspoon salt
5 cups flour
1 cup buttermilk (whole milk can be substituted)

In a bowl, mix together the shortening, sugar and molasses. In another bowl, sift together the soda, ginger, cinnamon, cloves, nutmeg, salt and flour. Combine the wet ingredients (including the buttermilk) and dry ingredients to create a soft dough.

Chill the dough for about an hour. Roll into a log and cut into disks. Place disks on a cookie sheet and sprinkle sugar on top. Bake at 375ºF for 10 to 15 minutes depending on how thick you cut the cookies.

Skye Suter has been involved with art and plants for most of her life. She worked at a newspaper as an Art Director. She also wrote garden and food columns. Skye worked at a botanical garden and for other non-profits in marketing and producing graphic design and educational programming.

Currently she is a freelance illustration instructor, a writer, a food correspondent, an illustrator and graphic artist for independent projects such as the International Herb Association's Herb of the Year books, and contract design projects.

HEALING & BEAUTY WITH GINGER

Ginger decoction with fresh Meyer lemon.
Susan Belsinger

Preserving sliced, fresh ginger rhizomes by dehydrating.
Susan Belsinger

THE MEDICINAL USES OF GINGER (ZINGIBER OFFICINALE) [ZINGIBERACEAE]

Daniel Gagnon

Medical Herbalist RH (AHG)

Other Common Names:
 Ayurvedic: *Ardraka* (fresh rhizome); *shunthi* (dried rhizome)
 Chinese: Pinyin: *jiang*; sheng jiang (fresh rhizome); *gan jiang* (dried rhizome); *pao jiang* (prepared rhizome); *jiang pi* (peel)
 Dutch: *Gember*
 English: Ginger; Some commercial grades were known as African ginger, cochin ginger, bleached Jamaica ginger, Calcutta ginger, Calicut ginger
 French: *Gingembre*
 German: *Ingwer*
 Italian: *Zenzero*
 Latin: *Zingiberis rhizoma*
 Japanese: *Shōga*
 Spanish: *Gengibre*; In Southwestern U.S.: *Ajengibre*

When Hippocrates wrote "Let food be your medicine and medicine be your food," he might have been thinking about ginger.

Ginger is an excellent example of a food being a powerful medicine and vice versa. Today, ginger is almost as important medicinally as it is culinarily. As you read this article and learn about ginger's benefits, keep in mind where you may incorporate this powerful herb into your diet and your everyday health regimen. Your body, mind, and soul will thank you for doing so.

Part used: The part of the ginger plant used in herbal medicine is named the rhizome. However, consumers refer to it as ginger root. For simplicity's sake, this paper will refer to the rhizome as the root.

Good quality ginger has a penetrating and very aromatic scent. The root should taste spicy, hot, and biting. These properties are quickly lost when the ground root is exposed to air (Grieve 1971). It is next to impossible to assess how long ginger powder found in the jars at the grocery store or in the bulk jars at natural food stores has been ground prior to purchase. Fresh root or whole dried root grated as needed is the ideal way to access the full medicinal value of ginger.

Herbal Properties: Ginger has a multitude of medicinal properties including antiallergic, antiarthritic, antibacterial, anticholesterol, antiemetic, antifever, antiflatulent, antihistaminic, anti-inflammatory, antioxidant, antiplatelet, antitussive, carminative, diaphoretic, digestive stimulant, expectorant, hepatoprotective (fresh), hypoglycemic, hypotensive, hypertensive, immunostimulant, peripheral circulatory stimulant, spasmolytic and stomachic activities (Bone 2013, Duke 2003, Hoffmann 2003, Leung 1996).

Constituents: More than 400 constituents have been identified in ginger root. It has been reported to contain from 0.25-3.3%

volatile oil, including zingiberene, curcumene, sesquiphellan-drene, and beta-bisabolene (Leung 1996). Since fresh ginger contains higher levels of zingiberene and sesquiphellandrene compared to dry ginger, it may explain why traditional Chinese medicine practitioners favor fresh ginger root in the treatment of colds (Denyer 1994).

Ginger also contains two major types of pungent principles: gingerols and shogaols. Shogaols are twice as pungent (hot) as gingerols and are produced when good quality roots are dried and stored properly or during the production of the oleoresin. Thus, dried ginger with its shogaols is more pungent or hot than fresh ginger (Wren 1988). Ginger contains 6 to 8% lipids and is composed of glycerides, lecithin, and free fatty acids including lauric, linoleic, oleic, palmitic, and stearic fatty acids. Other constituents include about 9% proteins; up to 50% starch; some vitamins including vitamin A and niacin (B3); minerals; diverse amino acids; and many other constituents (Bone 2013, Duke 2003, Leung 1996). A proteolytic enzyme (an enzyme that breaks down proteins) has been identified and is present at levels of 2.2% of the fresh rhizome (Duke 2003).

A Brief History of Ginger

Ginger is a native of Southeast Asia. The plant is mentioned in Chinese and Ayurvedic medicine texts dating back to 2000 BCE (Foster 1992). Ginger was used for digestive issues as well as for inflammation and rheumatism. The medicinal use of ginger in Europe can be traced back to Greek and Roman times (Heinrich 2004). It was introduced in Europe via the Red Sea.

During Antiquity and the Middle Ages, ginger was one of the most valued herbal medicines and among the most used spices in cooking. Dioscorides, a Greek physician and botanist, reported that candied ginger was imported to Europe through Italy and used to stimulate digestion, soothe the belly, and clear up vision. It was also used as medicine during medieval times. Hildegard of Bingen, a German Benedictine abbess and medical writer of the late Middle Ages, included ginger in her medicinal recipes for its tonic and antiseptic properties (Leclerc 1983).

Ginger was first introduced to Jamaica in 1525. It is reported that, as early as 1547, it became a major ginger producer, exporting more than 2 million pounds of the roots annually. For over four centuries, it was believed that the best ginger in the world originated from Jamaica (Lancashire 2014).

Today, ginger is cultivated in moist, warm tropical climates such as India, Nigeria, China, Nepal, and Indonesia. These five nations grow the majority of the ginger consumed worldwide (Wren 1988, *NationMaster* 2022). India is currently the top ginger root-growing nation in the world, producing a phenomenal 1,788,000 metric tons in 2019 and supplying 43% of the world's ginger roots (*NationMaster* 2022). Most of the cultivated varieties of ginger are sterile and do not flower. Of the varieties of cultivated plants that do flower, their seeds are often sterile (Mahr 2022).

Differentiating between Fresh, Dry, and Pan-fried Ginger

Ginger is a traditional ingredient used in many herbal formulas. It is used as an ingredient in nearly half of all the Traditional Chinese Medicine (TCM) multi-herb formulations (Foster 1992). In TCM, fresh root, dried root, and pan-fried ginger root are treated as three different medicines. Each one delivers its unique properties to a person's distinctive health condition (Leon 2017, Sionneau 1995).

Fresh ginger root (*sheng jiang*) is used to disperse colds and flu, reduce fevers, warm the stomach, ease or stop abdominal distension, stop vomiting, transform and expel phlegm, and stop coughs. It's also used to stop food poisoning due to crab and fish (Chen 2001). Research has shown that ginger effectively destroys anisakis larvae and other parasites found in raw fish (Bartram 1998).

Dried ginger root (*gan jiang*) is used for diarrhea, abdominal pain, cold limbs, lumbago (aka lower back pain), rheumatic pain, loss of appetite, and asthma with cough due to accumulation of phlegm in the lungs, especially when accompanied with excessive, clear, and thin mucus (Sionneau 1995).

The third type of ginger root is pan-fried dried ginger (*pao jiang*). It is used for excessive menstrual bleeding as well as diarrhea with abdominal pain (Sionneau 1995).

The Medicinal Properties of Ginger

Ginger root is highly valued in herbal medicine. Here are eight areas where it supports well- being and provides relief in health challenges.

Ginger and its antinausea and antiemetic properties

In the last 40 years, there has been a growing trend in studying ginger root as a remedy for seasickness, motion sickness, nausea, vomiting, and vertigo (White 2007). One of the major reasons ginger root is being studied so extensively for its antinausea and antiemetic properties is that conventional antiemetic drugs have potential teratogenic (substances that may cause developmental malformations) effects in pregnancy during the early growth period of the fetus (Jewell 2003).

This significant side effect of conventional drugs has fueled a keen interest in finding remedies that are devoid of side effects. Enter ginger. It has been safely used for nausea and vomiting for thousands of years (Mustafa 1990).

Results of studies show that ginger delivers on its promises, as many clinical trials show positive effects in morning sickness (Mowrey1982, Grontved 1988, British Herbal Compendium 1992). It is also an effective remedy for persistent, severe vomiting (hyperemesis gravidarum) during pregnancy (Fischer-Rasmusen 1990). A systematic review confirmed that ginger is an effective treatment of nausea and vomiting during pregnancy and reaffirmed the absence of side effects when ginger is used for this purpose (Borelli 2005).

Many clinical trials have been done on ginger root's effectiveness and safety not only during pregnancy (Vutyanavich 2001) but also in situations where nausea and vomiting are best avoided, such as in postoperative situations (Chaiyakunapruk 2006) and chemotherapy-induced nausea (Lete 2016). Ginger has been shown to be helpful in postoperative nausea and vomiting after major gynecological surgery (Bone 1990).

Several studies have demonstrated that ginger reduces or eliminates motion sickness. One such clinical trial revealed that ginger root was more effective than the antihistamine dimenhydrinate (Dramamine°) in reducing motion sickness. The authors of this trial explained that the aromatic and carminative properties of ginger ameliorate the effects of motion sickness in the gastrointestinal tract itself. Ginger may effectively block negative gastrointestinal reactions and subsequent nausea feedback (Mowrey 1982). In another motion sickness study, pretreatment with ginger (1,000 and 2,000 mg) reduced nausea considerably. Ginger also prolonged the time it took for volunteers to develop nausea and shortened the recovery time of motion sickness (Lien 2003). Ginger should be taken 2 to 4 hours before being subjected to motion that may trigger nausea and vomiting.

Some studies have reported that ginger had little to no effects on nausea or vomiting (Wood 1988, Stewart 1991). However, it is worth noting that most of the negative studies did not confirm the quality of the ginger medicine used in their clinical trials.

It is a well-known fact that the amounts of ginger's active constituents vary greatly depending on numerous factors. Factors such as how ginger root is dried, how long it has been dried, as well as how long it has been powdered prior to being used as a medicine have tremendous impact on clinical results. The bottom line is that the weight of the scientific evidence clearly demonstrates that ginger is beneficial in seasickness, motion sickness, pregnancy-induced nausea and vomiting, and chemotherapy-induced nausea as well as post-operative nausea and vomiting (White 2007, Ernst 2000, Jewell 2003).

Ginger and the digestive system

From the mouth to the large intestine, ginger offers invaluable help to the whole digestive system. Ginger's effects start in the mouth. It increases saliva secretion. This is critically important to set up proper digestive function (Bone 2013). Ginger is used to promote secretion of gastrointestinal juices, specifically hydrochloric acid, a very useful effect when the digestive system is acting sluggishly (Menzies-Trull 2003). Fresh root infusions produce a stimulant action on gastric secretion (Wu 2008). Ginger has been shown to stimulate the emptying of a "lazy" stomach and to reduce the risk of gastro-esophageal reflux in susceptible individuals (Priest 1983). The fresh root contains a proleolytic enzyme that increases protein digestion (Thompson 1973). Ginger also increases the production of bile (Yamahara 1985).

These beneficial effects on the digestive system explain why it is often used in the elderly and in individuals who produce too little digestive juice (achlorhydria or gastric subacidity) (Bartram 1998). For both groups, their main challenge is that insufficient digestive juices are secreted at mealtime to properly digest their meal and facilitate the timely transit of food through the intestines.

Further down the digestive tract, ginger stimulates healthy gastrointestinal motility. Ginger has a carminative effect on the digestive system. It reduces the production of gas through the activation of digestive enzyme production. It also relieves the intestinal pressure that occurs when gas accumulates in the intestines (Lohsiriwat 2010). Ginger may not be a one-minute miracle worker, but used regularly, it enhances digestion in people with low digestive fire. One interesting aspect of ginger is its ability to simultaneously improve gastric motility and exert antispasmodic effects (Pizzorno 2006). Ginger helps move food through the gastrointestinal system in a coordinated way and helps prevent spasms. Ginger root is known to reduce gas, flatulence, painful spasms, and diarrhea from over-relaxation of the digestive tract (Priest 1983). It delivers a tonic and antispasmodic action on intestinal tissue.

These positive gastrointestinal effects explain why ginger is often used for colic accompanied with extensive gas, irritable bowel, and diarrhea with little intestinal inflammation. It excels in uncomplicated stomach and intestinal problems, appetite loss, digestive uneasiness, and hiccups (Bartram 1998). When sluggish digestion becomes an ongoing health issue and the individual feels bloated or experiences a sense of fullness after meals, ginger is an herb that makes a significant difference. Frequent burps, minor cramps, heartburn, nausea, tendencies toward chronic diarrhea, sluggish bowels, irritable bowel syndrome, and constipation point to the need for ginger. Used regularly, ginger spells relief and well-being for sluggish digestive system sufferers.

Clinical studies have shown that ginger root is useful to prevent stomach or duodenal ulcers (Johji 1988, Skenderi 2003). Research points out that individuals who are under major stress can prevent gastric ulceration by using moderate amounts (1 to 2 grams) of fresh ginger root as a tisane (an infusion) on a daily basis (Yamahara 1990). Ginger's soothing and protective effects on the stomach and other mucous membranes may be increased by adding an equal amount of licorice (*Glycyrrhiza glabra*) root to the tea.

Ginger, like black pepper (*Piper nigrum*) and long pepper (*Piper longum*), stimulates the absorption of hard-to-absorb plant constituents and nutrients (Atal 1981). Researchers hypothesize that ginger may do so either by enhancing the absorption of constituents and nutrients in the gastrointestinal tract or by protecting herbal constituents from being metabolized too quickly by the liver. For individuals who experience difficulty in absorbing fat-soluble vitamins or nutrients, adding ginger to their diet can be a boon to their health (Johri 1992).

However, a few individuals with sensitive stomachs do not always tolerate the use of ginger (Weiss 1988). It may leave them with an unpleasant burning sensation. Fresh ginger in quantities of 5 grams or more per day may act as a gastric irritant and actually cause irritation of the stomach lining. Should this occur, reduce and keep the dosage of ginger to less than 4 grams per day.

Ginger and women's health

Ginger has long been considered a woman's friend. It is one of the best remedies when the uterus is said to be "cold". Symptoms of a "cold" uterus include delayed, scanty, or lack of menstruation with constant cramps, dull red clots, and a feeling of chilliness (Holmes 1989). Ginger stimulates and warms the uterus, promotes the healthy flow of menses, and prevents uterine spasms. The warming properties of dry ginger make it useful for period pains, especially when these are improved by the application of heat or ingestion of warm drinks. Freshly-ground dried ginger root prepared as a tea is excellent for menstrual cramps.

It's not only the warming qualities of ginger that improve the pain. The pungent constituents (gingerols and shogaols) of dried ginger deliver significant pain-relieving effects by inhibiting the activity of the prostaglandins and thromboxanes inflammatory compounds (Pole 2006). Taking 800 mg of quality ginger root every 3 to 4 hours has been shown to be as effective as conventional menstrual pain killers (Trickey 1998). One study found that after two months of treatment, ginger was as effective in relieving menstrual cramps as mefenamic acid, a nonsteroidal anti-inflammatory drug (NSAID) often used to treat mild to moderate menstrual cramps (Ozgoli 2009).

Another study found that treatment of primary dysmenorrhea (cramping pains that comes before and during a period) in students taking ginger for 5 days had a statistically significant effect on relieving intensity and duration of pain (Rahnama 2012). Ginger can also be used for amenorrhea (absence of menstruation) that's a side effect of having a cold or being chilled (Skenderi 2003). Fresh ginger is useful for women who experience nausea and vomiting with their period (see *Ginger and its antinausea and antiemetic activities*, above) (Trickey 1998) while pan-fried dried ginger (*pao jiang*) is indicated for excessive menstrual bleeding (Sionneau 1995).

Ginger and migraine headaches

Ginger has been reported to have a beneficial effect in alleviating the pain and frequency of migraine headaches (Martins 2019). It has been suggested that inhibition of the activity of the inflammatory substances thromboxanes and prostaglandins provides an explanation for the traditional reputation that ginger holds for pain relief in migraines (Mustafa 1990). Dr. Mitchell, a naturopathic physician, reports that patients experience a decrease in frequency and duration of headaches, including cluster and migraine headaches, when using ginger. He suggests this may be the result of the blood dispersion and vascular normalization effects of ginger.

Shogaols, one of ginger's active constituents, have been shown to inhibit the release of substance P, a neurotransmitter associated with pain impulses. He recommends a dose of 5 to 40 drops of ginger tincture several times daily (Mitchell 2003). A 2014

Iranian clinical trial compared the effects of ginger and suma-triptan (a painkiller used in migraine) and reported that the two treatments were equally effective (Maghbooli 2014).

For sufferers of migraines, one of the most frequent go-to herbs is feverfew (*Tanacetum parthenium*) herb. Feverfew blocks the release of inflammatory mediators including serotonin and his-tamine, which cause vasodilation of blood vessels in the brain. Dilation of blood vessels is believed to be the precursor to the development of migraines. Feverfew contains constituents that cause vasoconstriction. When using feverfew, the amount of inhibition is greater than that achieved with the use of non-steroidal anti-inflammatory drugs (NSAIDS) like ibuprofen or naproxen.

However, from a Traditional Chinese Medicine point of view, feverfew is considered cold while ginger is considered hot. When used together, they appear to balance each other's prop-erties (Trickey 1998). Research has shown that ginger and fever-few used together offer excellent relief to migraine sufferers (Cady 2005, Cady 2011). Additionally, premenstrual and men-strual migraines can be helped by ginger, but not when these occur around menopause as ginger often aggravates hot flashes (Trickey 1998).

Ginger and the circulatory system

Fresh ginger is a classic herbal remedy for the person who suffers from cold hands and feet. It is useful for increasing poor circula-tion. The fresh root causes vasodilation of the superficial blood vessels and increases peripheral circulation to the skin, extrem-ities, and surface of the body. When a hot fresh ginger tea is ingested, the person feels invigorated from the increased blood circulation and quickly experiences a sense of warmth (Tillotson 2001). Studies suggest that the pungent constituents (gingerols and shogaols) of ginger are the substances that stimulate heat-regulating receptors throughout the body (Vagedes 2021).

While fresh ginger root has been shown to stimulate the circulation at the surface of the body, dried ginger root has a warming effect that is experienced deeper into the body. Herbalists suggest the action of dry ginger is centrally stimulating, warming, and more deeply felt (Pole 2006). It also explains why dried ginger is used in suppressed menstruations from cold (see *Ginger and Women's Health,* above) since colds that suppress the menses tend to be experienced deeper in the body (Bartram 1998).

Ginger has been shown to be protective of the circulatory system. Platelets are small, colorless cell fragments in the blood that form clots and prevent or stop bleeding. Clotting may be lifesaving when a person is cut or injured since it reduces blood loss. However, when clotting occurs uncontrolled inside the body, it may lead to strokes or heart attacks. One of the keys to protecting the circulatory system is to keep the blood flowing freely. Ginger is an important herb that has been shown to suppress the activation of platelets, thus inhibiting aggregation (Mitchell 2003). In contrast to aspirin, an over-the-counter drug used to reduce platelet aggregation, ginger has few side effects (Wang 2011).

It is well known that consuming substantial amounts of fats lead to increased platelet aggregation (clumping) which may contribute to strokes. In a study where large amounts of butter were consumed, ginger was shown to prevent platelets aggregation (Verma 1993). Another study showed that consuming dried ginger root decreased serum and hepatic cholesterol. It also stimulated the conversion of cholesterol to bile acids which are then excreted through the feces (Sambaiah 1991). A recent clinical study indicated that daily administration of 1,000 mg ginger root powder reduced elevated serum triglyceride concentration, which is a risk factor for cardiovascular disease (Tabibi 2016), while another study showed that ginger has excellent antihyperlipidemic effects (Bhandari 1998). These studies reveal that ginger may protect the cardiovascular system. Individuals who suffer from high cholesterol levels, high blood pressure, diabetes, and obesity may consider adding 2 to 4 grams of ginger per day to their diet.

Ginger, cancer, and being chronically cold

A commonly reported side effect by cancer patients during or after treatment is heat-regulating issues. Many patients often experience ongoing feelings of being cold. Doctors refer to this treatment side effect as a "thermoregulation" issue. It creates quality-of-life problems, hidden costs arising from the need for extra heating, negative effects on the immune system, and an increased risk of developing sleep issues (Zadorozhna 2021). Oncologists and medical doctors have little to offer their patients to help them overcome these crippling issues. However, there is one herbal treatment that has delivered consistent results for these individuals. Clinical trials have shown that using a hot water footbath is a simple method to improve body warmth regulation, relieve symptoms of fatigue, improve sleep and immune system function as well as decrease pain intensity (Blazickova 2000, Yang 2010, Valizadeh 2015). A recent clinical trial demonstrated that when ginger root is added to these warm water footbaths, the patients experienced a prolonged warming effect.

The researchers theorized that the thermogenic effect may come about from the binding of ginger's active constituents, gingerols and shogaols, to thermoregulatory receptors located in the body. This therapy helps to relieve the cold sensation and discomfort experienced by the patients. Additionally, it has also been shown to help upregulate immune system function (up-regulate: to increase the sensitivity to a physiologically active substance) and is free of side effects (Vagedes 2021).

Ginger has also been reported to have substantial cancer preventive and antiproliferative properties when used as a food (Rhode 2007, Shukla 2007, Prasad 2015). Clinical research has shown that adding ginger as a supplement during chemotherapy decreased chemotherapy-induced nausea and lessened cancer-related fatigue (Marx 2013). These same researchers found that dividing a 1,200 mg dose of ginger into four doses a day (each capsule contained 300 mg of ginger standardized to 15 mg of gingerols) was more effective than taking the same amount of ginger once or twice a day (Marx 2017).

Ginger and seasonal ailments

Many people reach for ginger at the first sign of a cold, flu, sore throat, and other respiratory problems (Bartram 1995). The Chinese name *jiang* means *to defend*, suggesting that ginger helps to protect the body from dampness and cold (Foster 1992). Despite its warming properties, fresh ginger stimulates sweating, an action that helps reduce elevated body temperature and control fevers (Chevallier 2016). Not only does fresh ginger root make you sweat, it also stimulates your lungs to expel phlegm, relieves pain that comes with viral infections, and exhibits strong antiviral activity (Denyer 1994). Additionally, it is known to activate the immune system (Holmes 1989).

The diaphoretic (substance that increases perspiration) action of ginger makes it useful in viral colds (Pole 2006). Use fresh ginger at the onset of a cold or flu, especially when the person feels cold and is experiencing chills and fatigue (Holmes 1989). A cup of tea made with 1 scant teaspoon of freshly grated dry ginger root will often stop a cold or flu dead in its tracks when taken at the first signs of symptoms. The tea may be substituted with 60 drops of ginger root tincture in a cup of hot water. Repeat the dose every hour if the person is not sweating profusely from the first cup (Mitchell 2003). Once the pores of the skin are open and the person is sweating, the fever usually breaks (Hoffmann 1983). Ginger tea with honey may also be used as a gargle as it is effective in the relief of sore throat (Hoffmann 1983).

Ginger, inflammation, and arthritis

Inflammation is generated by substances called eicosanoids including prostaglandins, thromboxanes, and leukotrienes. Allergic reactions, arthritis, asthma, fever, migraines, rheumatoid arthritis, and a multitude of other symptoms and diseases occur as a result of inflammation (Hoffmann 2003). Inflammatory conditions such as arthritis and rheumatism often improve with the use of ginger (Trickey 1998). Levels of inflammatory substances, prostaglandins, thromboxanes, and leukotrienes, have been shown to decrease with the use of ginger (Grzanna 2005). Studies on ginger's action in rheumatic conditions have shown a moderately beneficial effect (Heinrich 2004). In one study, ginger alleviated pain and swelling in 75% of the patients with arthritis and 100 percent of patients with muscular discomfort.

The recommended dosage was 500 to 1,000 mg per day. However, many patients took three to four times the amount. Patients taking the higher dosages reported quicker and better relief (Srivastava 1992). Ginger can also be prepared as a liniment for external use. It is used as the base of many fibrositis (formerly known as fibromyalgia) and muscle sprain treatments (Hoffmann 1983).

How to Use Ginger as Medicine

Internally: Make a tea from the recently grated fresh or dried ginger root; 1 teaspoon to each cup of boiling water; let it sit/ infuse for 5 minutes, covered. Filter. Use 1 cup two to three times a day (Bartram 1998). A teaspoon of fresh ginger weighs about 2 grams, while a teaspoon of dried ginger weighs about 3 grams (Wichtl 2004).

Herbal extract made with 50% alcohol: Take 30 to 40 drops three times a day (morning, noon, and night) with meals (Wren 1988).

Tablets/capsules: Two 250 to 400 mg up to 4 times a day (Bartram 1998, Trickey 1998).

In almost all cases, follow this suggested use for at least one month and continue, if results are encouraging (Bartram 1998).

Externally: Infuse two teaspoons (4 grams) of grated fresh ginger root per cup of hot water for 10 minutes. Use as a compress in case of scalp seborrheic issues (cradle cap) in children (Raynaud 2007). Use as a compress for skin diseases of all kinds, as well as hemorrhoids (Valnet 1992). Use as a foot bath for cold sensations (for thermoregulation issues) and to enhance immune system function. Infuse 2 tablespoons of freshly ground dried ginger root in a gallon of hot water, let cool to body temperature, and soak feet for 10 minutes. Stop the foot bath if or when the person feels uncomfortable (Vagedes 2021).

Safety: There are no safety concerns surrounding the use of this herb. The *Botanical Safety Handbook* classifies Ginger as a **Class 1** herb, an herb that can be safely consumed when used appropriately (Gardner 2013). Some practitioners believe that using ginger may reduce the effect of antacids as it increases gastric secretions (Bone 2013).

Pregnancy: Based on traditional Chinese medicine, it is suggested that pregnant women take no more than 2 grams of dried ginger root on a daily basis (Chen 2001, Bone 2003, Hoffmann 2003, Bensky 2004).

Contraindications: In Ayurvedic medicine, ginger is contraindicated for high *pitta* individuals, people that tend to run "hot." In these individuals, it has a tendency to aggravate heartburn, ulcers, and sweating (Pole 2006).

Side Effects: Gastrointestinal symptoms, such as heartburn, are occasionally associated with ginger use, especially with large doses of ginger (Gardner 2013). Excessive doses of preparations made from fresh ginger have been reported to cause dry mouth, sore throat, nosebleeds, and kidney inflammation (Bensky 2004).

Drug Interactions: The *Botanical Safety Handbook* has classified ginger as an **Interaction Class B** herb: "an herb for which clinically relevant interactions are biologically plausible" (Gardner 2013). This rating was based on a human trial that indicated that the hypertension and angina medication nifedipine taken with ginger had a greater antiplatelet action than nifedipine alone (Young 2006).

References

Atal, CK., Zutshi, U., Rao, PG. 1981. "Scientific evidence of the role of Ayurvedic herbals on bioavailability of drugs." *J. Ethnopharmacol,* 4(2): 229-232.

Bartram, T. 1998. *Bartram's Encyclopedia of Herbal Medicine.* Constable & Robinson Ltd.

Bensky, D. Clavey, C., and E. Stöger, E. 2004. *Chinese Herbal Medicine Materia Medica.* 3 ed., Eastland Press.

Bhandari, U., Sharma, J., and Zafar, R. 1998. "The protective action of ethanolic ginger (*Zingiber officinale*) extract in cholesterol fed rabbits." *Journal of Ethnopharmacology,* 61(2): 167–171.

Blazickova, S., Rovensky, J., Koska, J., and Vigas, M. 2000. "Effect of hyperthermic water bath on parameters of cellular immunity." *Int J Clin Pharmacol Res,* 20(1-2): 41-46.

Bone, K. (2003) *A Clinical Guide to Blending Liquid Herbs.* Elsevier Churchill Livingstone.

Bone. K. and Mills, S. (2013). *Principles and Practice of Phytotherapy,* 2 ed. Churchill Livingstone.

Bone, ME., Wilkinson, DJ., Young, JR., McNeil, MB., and Charlton, MB. 1990. "Ginger root - a new antiemetic. The effect of ginger root on postoperative nausea and vomiting after major gynaecological surgery." *Anaesthesia,* 45: 669-671

Borrelli, F., Capasso, R., Aviello, G., Pittler, M. H., and Izzo, AA. 2005. "Effectiveness and Safety of Ginger in the Treatment of Pregnancy-Induced Nausea and Vomiting." *Obstetrics & Gynecology,* 105(4): 849–856.

The British Herbal Compendium. 1992. British Herbal Medical Association.

Cady, R. K., Goldstein, J., Nett, R., Mitchell, R., Beach, M. E., and Browning, R. 2011. "A Double-Blind Placebo-Controlled Pilot Study of Sublingual Feverfew and Ginger (LipiGesicTMM) in the Treatment of Migraine." *Headache: The Journal of Head and Face Pain*, 51(7): 1078–1086.

Cady, RK., Schreiber, CP., Beach, ME., and Hart, CC. 2005. "Gelstat Migraine (sublingually administered feverfew and ginger compound) for acute treatment of migraine when administered during the mild pain phase." *Med Sci Monit*, 11: I65–I69.

Chaiyakunapruk, N., Kitikannakorn, N., Nathisuwan, S., Leeprakobboon, K., and Leelasettagool, C. 2006. "The efficacy of ginger for the prevention of postoperative nausea and vomiting: A meta-analysis." *American Journal of Obstetrics and Gynecology*, 194(1): 95–99.

Chen J, and T. Chen. 2001. *Chinese Medical Herbology and Pharmacology*. Art of Medicine Press, Inc.

Chevallier, A. 2016. *Encyclopedia of Herbal Medicine*. 3 ed., Dorling Kindersley Limited.

Denyer, C. V., Jackson, P., Loakes, D. M., Ellis, M. R., and Young, D. A. B. 1994. "Isolation of Antirhinoviral Sesquiterpenes from Ginger (*Zingiber officinale*)." *Journal of Natural Products*: 57(5): 658–662.

Duke, J. 2003, *Handbook of Medicinal Spices*. CRC Press.

Ernst, E., and Pittler, M. H. 2000. "Efficacy of ginger for nausea and vomiting: a systematic review of randomized clinical trials." *British Journal of Anaesthesia*, 84(3): 367–371.

Fischer-Rasmussen, W., Kjær, S. K., Dahl, C., and Asping, U. 1991. "Ginger treatment of hyperemesis gravidarum." *European Journal of Obstetrics & Gynecology and Reproductive Biology*, 38(1): 19–24.

Gardner, Z. and McGuffin, M. editors. 2013. *Botanical Safety Handbook, 2 ed.*, CRC Press.

Grieve, M. 1971. *A Modern Herbal.* Dover Publications, Inc. (reprint of 1931 ed.).

Grøntved, A., Brask, T., Kambskard, J., & Hentzer, E. 1988. "Ginger Root Against Seasickness: A Controlled Trial on the Open Sea." *Acta Oto-Laryngologica,* 105(1-2): 45–49.

Grzanna, R., Lindmark, L., and Frondoza, C. G. 2005. "Ginger —An Herbal Medicinal Product with Broad Anti-Inflammatory Actions." *Journal of Medicinal Food,* 8(2): 125–132.

Foster, S. and Chongxi, Y. 1992. *Herbal Emissaries.* Healing Arts Press.

Heinrich, M., Barnes, J., Gibbons, S. and Williamson, EM. 2004. *Fundamentals of Pharmacognosy and Phytotherapy.* Churchill Livingstone.

Holmes, P. 1989. *The Energetic of Western Herbs.* Artemis Press.

Hoffmann, D. 1983. *The New Holistic Herbal.* Element Books Limited.

Hoffmann, D. 2003. *Medical Herbalism.* Healing Arts Press.

Jewell, D., and Young, G. 2003. "Interventions for nausea and vomiting in early pregnancy." *Cochrane Database of Systematic Reviews.*

Johji, Y., Michihiko, M., Huang Qi Rong, Hisashi, M., and Hajime, F. 1988. "The anti-ulcer effect in rats of ginger constituents." *Journal of Ethnopharmacology,* 23(2-3): 299–304.

Johri, R. K., and Zutshi, U. 1992. "An Ayurvedic formulation 'Trikatu' and its constituents." *Journal of Ethnopharmacology,* 37(2): 85–91.

Lancashire, RJ. 2014. "Jamaican Ginger." http://wwwchem.uwimona.edu.jm/lectures/ginger.html. Accessed on 8/31/2022.

Leclerc, H. 1929. *Les Épices.* Paris, France: Masson. (First published in 1929).

Leon, C. and Yu-Lin, L. 2017. *Chinese Medicinal Plants, Herbal Drugs and Substitutes*. Kew Publishing.

Lete, I., and Allué, J. 2016. "The Effectiveness of Ginger in the Prevention of Nausea and Vomiting during Pregnancy and Chemotherapy." *Integrative Medicine Insights*. 11: IMI.S36273.

Leung, A. and S. Foster. 1996. *Encyclopedia of Common Natural Ingredients used in Food, Drugs and Cosmetics*. 2 ed., John Wiley & Sons, Inc.

Lien, HC., Sun, WM., Chen, YH., Kim, H., Hasler, W. and Owyang, C.2003. "Effects of ginger on motion sickness and gastric slow-wave dysrhythmias induced by circular vection." *Am J Physiol Gastrointest Liver Physiol,* 284: 481–489.

Lohsiriwat, S., Rukkiat, M., Chaikomin, R., Leelakusolvong, S. 2010. "Effect of ginger on lower esophageal sphincter pressure." *J Med Assoc Thai,* (93)3: 366-372.

Maghbooli, M., Golipour, F., Moghimi Esfandabadi, A., and Yousefi, M. 2014. "Comparison Between the Efficacy of Ginger and Sumatriptan in the Ablative Treatment of the Common Migraine." *Phytotherapy Research,* 28(3): 412–415.

Mahr, S. 2022. Ginger, *Zingiber officinale.* Wisconsin Horticulture, Division of Extension, University of Wisconsin – Madison. https://hort.extension.wisc.edu/ articles/ginger-zingiber-offici- nale/#:~:text=Container%20grown%20plants%20rarely%20flowe r,stem%20from%20the%20foliage%20stem. Accessed on 9-4-2022.

Martins, L. B., Rodrigues, A. M. dos S., Rodrigues, D. F., dos Santos, L. C., Teixeira, A. L., and Ferreira, A. V. M. 2019. "Double-blind placebo-controlled randomized clinical trial of ginger (*Zingiber officinale* Rosc.) addition in migraine acute treatment." *Cephalalgia,* 39(1): 68-76.

Marx, W. M., Teleni, L., McCarthy, A. L., Vitetta, L., McKavanagh, D., Thomson, D., and Isenring, E. 2013. "Ginger (*Zingiber officinale*) and chemotherapy-induced nausea and vomiting: a systematic literature review." *Nutrition Reviews,* 71(4): 245–254.

Marx, W., McCarthy, A., Ried, K., McKavanagh, D., Vitetta, L., Sali, A., Lohning, A., and Isenring, E. 2017. "The Effect of a Standardized Ginger Extract on Chemotherapy-Induced Nausea-Related Quality of Life in Patients Undergoing Moderately or Highly Emetogenic Chemotherapy: A Double Blind, Randomized, Placebo Controlled Trial." *Nutrients,* 9(8): 867-880.

McGuffin, M., Kartesz, J.F., Leung, AY. and Tucker, A.O. 2000. *Herbs of Commerce.* 2 ed., American Herbal Products Association.

Menzies-Trull, C. 2003. *Herbal Medicine, Keys to Physiomedicalism including Pharmacopoeia.* Faculty of Physiomedical Herbal Medicine.

Mitchell, W. 2003. *Plant Medicine in Practice.* Elsevier Science.

Moore, M. 1990. *Los Remedios: Traditional Herbal Remedies of the Southwest.* Museum of New Mexico Press.

Mowrey, D., and Clayson, D. 1982. "Motion sickness, ginger, and psychophysics." *The Lancet.* 319(8273): 655–657.

Mustafa, T., & Srivastava, K. C. 1990. "Ginger (*Zingiber officinale*) in migraine headache." *Journal of Ethnopharmacology,* 29(3): 267–273.

"Ginger Production." *NationMaster.* https://www.nationmaster.com/nmx/ranking/ginger-production. Accessed 9-5-2022.

Ozgoli, G., Goli, M., and Moattar, F. 2009. "Comparison of Effects of Ginger, Mefenamic Acid, and Ibuprofen on Pain in Women with Primary Dysmenorrhea." *The Journal of Alternative and Complementary Medicine,* 15(2): 129–132.

Pizzorno, J, and M. Murray. 2006. *Textbook of Natural Medicine.* 3 ed., Churchill Livingstone Elsevier.

Pole, S. 2006. *Ayurvedic Medicine: The Principles of Traditional Practice*. Philadelphia, PA: Churchill Livingstone Elsevier.

Prasad, S., and Tyagi, AK. 2015. "Ginger and Its Constituents: Role in Prevention and Treatment of Gastrointestinal Cancer." *Gastroenterology Research and Practice*.

Priest, AW. and Priest, LR. 1983. *Herbal Medication*. Essex, UK: The C.W. Daniel Company Ltd.

Rahnama, P., Montazeri, A., Huseini, H. F., Kianbakht, S., and Naseri, M. 2012. "Effect of *Zingiber officinale* R. rhizomes (ginger) on pain relief in primary dysmenorrhea: a placebo randomized trial." *BMC Complementary and Alternative Medicine*, 12(1): 92-100.

Raynaud, J. 2007. *Prescriptions et conseils en phytothérapie*. Lavoisier.

Rhode, J., Fogoros, S., Zick, S., Wahl, H., Griffith, K., Huang, J. and Liu, R. 2007. "Ginger inhibits cell growth and modulates angiogenic factors in ovarian cancer cells." *Complementary and Alternative Medicine Research*, 7: 44-53.

Sambaiah, K. Srinivasan, K. 1991. "Effect of cumin, cinnamon, ginger, mustard andtamarind in induced hypercholesterolemic rats." *Die Nahrung*, 35(1): 47-51.

Shukla, Y., & Singh, M. (2007). "Cancer preventive properties of ginger: A brief review." *Food and Chemical Toxicology*, 45(5): 683–690.

Sionneau, P. 1995. *An Introduction to the Use of Processed Chinese Medicinals*. Translated by Bob Flaws. Blue Poppy Press.

Skenderi, G. 2003. *Herbal Vade Mecum*. Herbacy Press.

Srivastava, K. C., and Mustafa, T. (1992). "Ginger (*Zingiber officinale*) in rheumatism and musculoskeletal disorders." *Medical Hypotheses*, 39(4): 342–348.

Stewart, J. J., Wood, M. J., Wood, C. D., and Mims, M. E. 1991. "Effects of Ginger on Motion Sickness Susceptibility and Gastric Function." *Pharmacology*, 42(2): 111–120.

Tabibi, H., Imani, H., Ataback, S., Najafi, I., Hedayati, M., and Rahmani L. 2016. "Effects of ginger on serum lipids and lipoproteins in peritoneal dialysis patients: A randomized controlled trial." *Peritoneal Dialysis International,* 36: 140–145.

Thompson, EH., Wolf, ID., and Allen, CE. 1973. "Ginger rhizome: A new source of proteolytic enzyme." *Journal of Food Science,* 38(4): 652-655.

Tillotson, AK. 2001. *The One Earth Herbal Sourcebook.* Kensington Books.

Trickey, R. 1998. *Women, Hormones & Menstrual Cycle.* Allen & Unwin.

Uphof, J.C. 1968. *Dictionary of Economic Plants.* Stechert-Harner Service Agency, Inc.

Vagedes, J., Hiller, S., Kuderer, S., Vagedes, K., Szoeke, H., and Wolf, U. 2021. "Examining the efficacy of mustard and ginger footbaths to increase warmth in oncological patients: a randomized controlled trial." *European Journal of Integrative Medicine,* 48.

Valizadeh, L., Seyyedrasooli, A., Zamanazadeh, V., and Nasiri, K. 2015. "Comparing the effects of reflexology and footbath on sleep quality in the elderly: a controlled clinical trial." *Iran Red Crescent Med J,* 17(11): e20111.

Valnet, J. 1992. Phytothérapie. 6 ed. Maloine. Van Hellemont, J. 1986. *Compendium de Phytothérapie.* Association Pharmaceutique Belge.

Verma, SK, Singh, J., Khamesra, R., and Bordia, A. 1993. "Effect of ginger on platelet aggregation in man." *Indian J Med Res,* 98: 240-242.

Vutyavanich, T., and Kraiarin, T. 2001. "Ginger for nausea and vomiting in pregnancy: Randomized, double-masked, placebo-controlled trial." *Obstetrics & Gynecology:* 97(4): 577–582.

Wang, Z., Hasegawa, J., Wang, X., Matsuda, A., Tokuda, T. Miura, N., and Watanabe, T. 2011. "Protective effects of ginger against aspirin-induced gastric ulcers in rats." *Yonago Acta Med*, 54(1): 11-19.

Weiss, R. 1988. *Herbal Medicine*. Beaconsfield Publishers Ltd.

White, B. 2007. "Ginger: an overview." *Am Fam Physician* 75(11): 1689-1691.

Wichtl, M. (Ed.) 2004. *Herbal Drugs and Phytopharmaceuticals*. 3 ed., CRC Press.

Wood, C. D., Manno, J. E., Wood, M. J., Manno, B. R., and Mims, M. E. 1988. "Comparison of Efficacy of Ginger with Various Antimotion Sickness Drugs." *Clinical Research Practices and Drug Regulatory Affairs*, 6(2): 129–136.

Wren, RB. 1988. *Potter's New Cyclopaedia of Botanical Drugs and Preparations*. Revised by E. Williamson. The C.W. Daniel Company Limited.

Wu, KL., Rayner, CK, Chuah, SK., Changchien, CS., Lu,SN., Chiu, YC., Chiu, KW., Lee, CM. 2008. "Effects of ginger on gastric emptying and motility in healthy humans." *Eur J Gastroenterol Hepatol*, 20(5): 436-440.

Yang HL, Chen XP, Lee KC, Fang FF, Chao YF. 2010. "The effects of warm-water footbath on relieving fatigue and insomnia of the gynecologic cancer patients on chemotherapy." *Cancer Nurs*, 33: 454-460.

Yamahara J., Miki, K., Chisaka, T., Sawada, T., Fujimura, H., Tomimatsu, T., Nakano, K., and Nohara, T. 1985. "Cholagogic effect of ginger and its active constituents." *J Ethnopharmacol*, 13(2): 217-225.

Yamahara, J., Huang, Q., Li, Y., Xu, L., and Fujimura, H. 1990. "Gastrointestinal Motility Enhancing Effect of Ginger and Its Constituents." *Chem Farm Bull*, 38(2): 430-431.

Young, H.-Y., Liao, J.-C., Chang, Y.-S., Luo, Y.-L., Lu, M.-C., and Peng, W.-H. 2006. "Synergistic Effect of Ginger and Nifedipine on Human Platelet Aggregation: A Study in Hypertensive

Patients and Normal Volunteers." *The American Journal of Chinese Medicine,* 34(04): 545–551.

Zadorozhna, M., and Mangieri, D. 2021. "Mechanisms of Chemopreventive and Therapeutic Proprieties of Ginger Extracts in Cancer." *Int. J. Mol. Sci,* 22(12): 6599.

Daniel Gagnon, *Medical Herbalist, MS, RH (AHG) is a French-Canadian originally from Northern Ontario who relocated to Santa Fe, NM in 1979. He has been a practicing Medical Herbalist since 1976. Daniel is the author of <u>The Practical Guide to Herbal Medicines</u>, a book designed to provide herbal health care options. With Amadea Morningstar, he is also the co-author of <u>Breathe Free</u>, a book on healing the respiratory system. He regularly teaches herbal therapeutics both nationally and internationally. Daniel is the owner of Herbs, Etc., an herbal medicine retail store and manufacturing facility, and can be reached at:*

botandan@aol.com.

Sliced ginger rhizome coins
Susan Belsinger

Dorene's Joint Ease Blend is easy to make using familiar ingredients--and it works! (I even put it in the bath.)

Susan Belsinger

GENEROUS GINGER
ESSENTIAL OIL

Dorene Petersen

Open generous ginger essential oil, and it wafts from the bottle with a sweet, peppery allure. This wonderful oil is loaded with potent health-giving aroma molecules packing a powerful wellness punch. Ginger, *Zingiber officinale* Roscoe, is from the family Zingiberaceae and is known as common ginger, Jamaican ginger, or ginger root. The Zingiberaceae plant family is rich with powerful essential oils and includes turmeric *Curcuma longa* L. and cardamom *Elettaria cardamomum* (L.) Maton.

The Greeks and Romans were onto something, as they highly valued ginger root traded by Arabian merchants via the Red Sea. It was introduced to France and Germany in the 9th century and a century later to England. Spanish conquistadors were responsible for taking ginger to the West Indies and Mexico, and as early as 1547, Jamaica exported ginger to Spain.

Paracelsus (1493-1541), who popularized the "Signatura doctrinae," now known as the Doctrine of Signatures,[1] identified

177

similarities between the shape of ginger and the human digestive system. Paracelsus was indeed very perceptive, as modern
research confirms ginger's support for the digestive system. In
the 12th century, Saint Hildegard referred to ginger as having
"aphrodisiac properties, especially for stimulating the vigor of
older men married to younger women."

According to the *Fragrance Raw Material Monographs* ginger essential oil has been in public use since before the 1900s.[2] Ginger
essential oil was approved in 1965 by the Food and Drug Administration (FDA) for food use and designated Generally Rec-
ognized as Safe (GRAS) status. Both the ginger essential oil and
the solvent-free ginger oleoresin, which is a naturally occurring
combination of the oil and resin, are listed on the GRAS list.[4]
Ginger is still used extensively in Chinese medicine.

The Fragrance Raw Material Monographs also state that the Council
of Europe in 1970 included ginger oil in the list of substances
permissible for use, with a possible limitation of the active prin-
ciple zingiberene in the final product.[3]

As a rule, essential oils should always be purchased only after
checking the specific Latin name. Ginger is no exception as it
can be confused with galangal, *Alpinia officinarum* Hance, also
from the Zingiberaceae family, and called ginger root or Chinese
ginger. While galangal has some traditional medicinal similarities, including being a Chinese Pharmacopoeia noted cure for
stomach aches,[5] the constituent profile of the essential oil is
very different from *Z. officinale.*

Ginger is cultivated in tropical and subtropical countries, such
as Jamaica, West Africa, China, Sierra Leone, India, Indonesia,
Vietnam, and Australia. There are many commercial varieties

of the root. The cultivar, geographical origin, maturity of the rhizome at harvest, agricultural and climatic conditions experienced during its growth cycle, the oil extraction process, and whether the rhizome is fresh or dried when distilled will all influence the composition of ginger oil and, subsequently, its aromatic profile. The oil is found mainly in the epidermal tissue of the rhizome. Jamaican ginger essential oil is the most sought-after for aromatherapy with a sweet peppery aromatic profile. Nigerian ginger essential oil is also considered to be a good option.

Ginger essential oil is usually produced from dried, whole rhizomes, fresh peelings, and shavings if used immediately. Fresh ginger is not traditionally used to make the oil; if used however, the final essential oil composition will be different. The dried rhizomes must be chopped or coarsely ground to expose more of the secretory cell surface to steam. The distillation waters may require cohobation or running the water through the distillation process again to remove all the oil. The yield is usually around 3%. A solvent extraction is also made with ground ginger, which produces a ginger absolute. Oleoresin contains the nonvolatile pungent principles that make ginger so unique. Ginger absolute is also made using a carbon dioxide (CO_2) extraction. Ginger CO_2 absolute is said to possess the most true-to-nature aroma of ginger. The solvent absolute, which may still contain residual solvents, is used more in perfumery. In contrast, the solvent-free CO_2 extract or oleoresin is used more in flavoring and aromatherapy treatments.

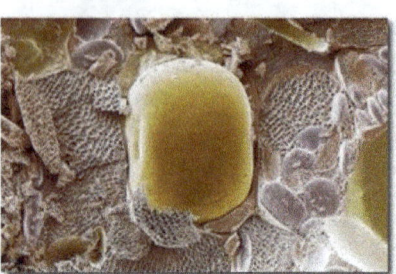

**Ginger rhizome, oil globule oozing
from secretory cell.**
©Image by Svoboda, K. & Svoboda, T. (2000).
Secretory Structures of Aromatic and Medicinal
Plants. Knighton, UK: Microscopix Publications.
Reproduced with permission.

Looking at the range of organoleptic and physical characteristics of an essential oil is a tried-and-true way to evaluate its quality. Organoleptic analysis reveals aspects using one or all of your senses. This means we look at the color, aroma, feel, and taste. The color is indicative to some extent of the geographical source. Ginger essential oil, according to the International Standards (ISO), can range in color from pale yellow to amber for Chinese ginger, yellow for Indian, and pale yellow to yellow for Nigerian.[6] Note that Jamaican and Madagascan ginger are sought after for aromatherapy and are not detailed in the ISO standards.

The aroma of ginger essential oil is a characteristic peppery, almost sweet lemony aroma, but not the intense flavor of the spice. Nigerian ginger has a heavy, oily, woody aroma. Ginger oil will become thicker or resinified (to make or become a resin or resin-like) if exposed to air over a period of time. When you rub the oil between your fingers, it should feel thin and dry quickly. If you drop a few drops on a perfume blotter, it should not leave a darkened stain.

Solubility in alcohol is another effective way to evaluate the quality of an essential oil. If it deviates from the standards, it reveals that it has been adulterated with an intentional or unintentional substance. Adulterated essential oils are best avoided. Ginger essential oil is only slightly soluble in 95% alcohol.

Other evaluation tests that require specialized equipment and expertise are specific gravity, optical rotation, and refractive index. Ginger essential oil has a specific gravity of 0.866 to 0.877 at 15°C, and the International Standards range for the refractive index at 20°C is 1.489 to 1.496, and the optical rotation range at 20°C is between -47° and -26° for Chinese, between -50° and -27° for Indian and between -47° and -18° for West African. These are considered accepted values and published by the ISO.[7] If the ginger essential oil you buy is sourced from outside these ISO-listed countries, ensure that the optical rotation and other physical characteristics fall within the lowest and highest of the given ranges.

Ginger essential oil distilled from fresh ginger rhizomes will contain more curcumene, which the ISO lists as ranging from 3 to 11%. The sesquiterpenes zingiberene, alpha-curcumene, bisabolone, and farnesene dominate ginger essential oil. Zingiberene is the primary marker constituent and is known as the ginger-specific sesquiterpene hydrocarbon. The range should be between 23 to 45%. The range is dependent on the geographical location, and it should always be present and at the recommended levels. Australian ginger consists of mainly monoterpenes, such as camphene, phellandrenecamphene, phellandrene, and alcohols, such as geraniol and linalool. Vietnamese ginger contains more geraniol and is similar to the Indian variety. Jamaican ginger contains the aldehydes, neral, decyl aldehyde, delta-camphene, phellandrene, cineole, borneol, geraniol, gingerol, gamma-eudesmol, linalool, citral, methyl heptenone, chavicol, a sesquiterpene, zingiberene, and zingiberol, a sesquiterpene alcohol that provides the mild, characteristic aroma.

While ginger essential oil has numerous notable therapeutic actions and medicinal uses, the antiemetic action is perhaps the best known. Motion and morning sickness are two uses that spring to our minds when we think of ginger for home use. However, it is important to differentiate between dried ginger root, whole or powdered, and ginger essential oil, particularly during pregnancy.

Nausea and vomiting continue to be significant issues that can severely impact health and recovery in a hospital setting,[8] while many pharmaceutical antiemetics can cause serious side effects. Researchers have been conducting clinical trials with ginger exploring the antinausea action in hospital settings for postoperative nausea and vomiting and for pre- and post-cancer infusion therapy where a non-pharmaceutical antiemetic is needed. An older 2005 study showed that a 5% application of ginger essential oil to patients' wrists before general anesthesia prevented nausea in approximately 80% of treated patients.[9]

In 2012 the Department of Anesthesia at the Carolinas Medical Center University, Charlotte, North Carolina, performed a randomized trial of aromatherapy for postoperative patients experiencing nausea. They were administered either an inhalation of ginger essential oil, an essential oil blend (ginger, peppermint *Mentha ×piperita* L., spearmint *Mentha spicata* L., and cardamom *Elettaria cardamomum* (L.) Maton, or isopropyl alcohol.

The number of antiemetic medications requested after aromatherapy was significantly reduced with ginger (P = 0.002) or aromatherapy blend (P < 0.001) versus saline. The researchers felt this confirmed aromatherapy as a viable treatment for postoperative nausea.[10]

Another study concluded that ginger-infused gauze pads provided nausea relief in approximately 67% of patients compared with 40% in the placebo group. Further, when ginger essential oil was blended with spearmint, peppermint, and cardamom, nausea relief increased to 82% of patients.[11] A randomized placebo-controlled study conducted in 2019 explored the treatment potential of using ginger, lavender, and rose essential oils versus placebo for postoperative nausea and vomiting in patients. While 5,205 patients who met the eligibility criteria were accepted into the trial, not all experienced postoperative nausea and vomiting. The trial finally included 184 patients, who were said to have an excellent sense of smell. Two drops of either ginger, lavender, rose oil, or pure water were dropped onto a gauze pad, and the patient was asked to inhale the aroma for 5 minutes. Nausea and vomiting scores were evaluated at 15 and again at 40 minutes after the oils were inhaled. Results were statistically evident at 15 minutes and more significant at 40 minutes, with ginger and lavender showing a substantial reduction in nausea and vomiting compared to rose and the placebo.[12]

The use of ginger as a treatment for chemotherapy-induced nausea is another area that researchers are exploring. Several recent clinical trials have evaluated the efficacy of inhaled ginger essential oil to reduce decreased appetite, anxiety, fatigue, and nausea during chemotherapy, specifically for neuroendocrine, skin, and gastrointestinal cancer.[13] [14]One of these studies compared ginger, German chamomile *Matricaria recutita* L., and bergamot *Citrus aurantium* var. *bergamia* Loisel, (synonym of *Citrus ×limon* (L.) Burm.fil) essential oils versus an odorless control oil on appetite, anxiety, fatigue, and nausea. The results showed ginger essential oil produced statistically significant results for anxiety and fatigue.[15] Furthermore, a systematic literature review suggested ginger may reduce nausea during chemotherapy in patients with breast cancer.

A total of nine clinical trials were included, which were published between 2012 and 2017.[16] The method of administration of ginger varied among trials and included delivery of two drops of ginger essential oil delivered via an aroma necklace; other studies gave capsules of 0.25 or 0.5 grams of dried ginger root or dried powdered ginger root containing specific constituent profiles; while another study administered 500 mg of powdered ginger twice daily, mixed with a spoonful of yogurt to make swallowing easier. The duration ranged from 3 to 10 days, and ginger was given five days before to 30 minutes after the beginning of chemotherapy.[17] One study speculated that initiating the ginger treatment protocol before chemotherapy starts resulted in a more significant reduction of chemotherapy-induced nausea.[18] However, further studies are needed to verify this claim.

A double-blind placebo trial in 2018 evaluating ginger essential oil in relieving chemotherapy-induced nausea in 21 children with cancer resulted in a 67% improvement. However, the researchers concluded that while ginger essential oil was well received, well tolerated, nontoxic, and noninvasive, it did not significantly decrease nausea in patients enrolled in this study.[19]

However, for anyone embarking on chemotherapy, it seems that starting treatment with ginger five days before chemotherapy begins may elicit better results. For anyone who cannot tolerate the taste or aroma of ginger, transdermal patches are another potential delivery method. Massage is another viable alternative. Researchers in a single-blind, randomized controlled trial demonstrated improved cellular immunity for patients receiving chemotherapy for bowel cancer who received three Thai massage sessions using ginger essential oil and coconut oil over one week. Lymphocyte numbers were boosted by 11%. As an added benefit, fatigue, pain, and stress were all reduced in the group receiving ginger essential oil massage compared to the control group.[20] Nausea was not mentioned in this study, however reduced stress and anxiety typically results in reduced nausea. Overall, the results of these studies showed that all forms of ginger, not just the essential oil, and all administration methods resulted in positive outcomes.

In the almost-post-pandemic world, depression and anxiety continue to manifest in all segments of the population. The World Health Organization (WHO) estimates the pandemic has triggered a 25% increase in anxiety and depression worldwide. Young people and women were said to be the hardest hit.[21] This overwhelming health crisis has manifested in many children and young adults with a marked increase in eating disorders such anorexia, bulimia and the less well-known subtype called avoidant restrictive food intake disorder (ARFID).[22] Even though ARFID was added to the psychiatric nomenclature in 2013, little is known about its optimal treatment.[23] Anxiety and nausea are associated with all types of eating disorders, but particularly with ARFID.[24] Controlling nausea and subsequent loss of appetite associated with anxiety is a challenge. An individualized inhaler of ginger, lavender, chamomile, and bergamot essential oils could offer symptomatic relief.

Ginger essential oil may not be the first oil that comes to mind when we look for antifungal and antimicrobial actions. However, a very early study showed that ginger essential oil demonstrated good antibacterial activity against *Staphylococcus aureus*.[25] A study in 2021 evaluated the potential for ginger and ginger essential oil in wound dressings.[26] A hydrogel nanofiber release of fatty acids results in an undesirable acidic pH. The researchers found that the addition of antioxidant-rich ginger oil not only minimizes the oxidation of soy lecithin, but also provides antibacterial, antimicrobial activity against both Gram (-) and Gram (+) bacteria.[27] Other studies have confirmed this antibacterial potential and reveal that ginger essential oils have the ability to inhibit *Escherichia coli* and *Staphylococcus aureus*.[28] The antibacterial activity of ginger essential oils is attributed to the constituents zingiberene, α-farnesene, 6-gingerol, and α-curcumene. Researchers have shown that these constituents attack microbial cell membranes and cell walls which causes intracellular components to leak from the cell resulting in cell death.[29]

The antifungal action of ginger is also of interest. Food-borne fungi such as *Fusarium moniliforme*, usually found in corn, are inhibited and destroyed by ginger essential oil and oleoresin.[30] If food infected with *Fusarium* is eaten by immune-compromised people[31], it can cause mycotoxicosis. An in-vitro study in 2008 showed ginger essential oil to be effective against several fluconazole-resistant strains of Candida yeasts.[32] Ginger reduced the growth and aflatoxin production of *Aspergillus parasiticus* when used in the concentration range of 100-300 ppm.[33]

For those with arthritis, ginger essential oil, oleoresin, and CO_2 extract have demonstrated anti-inflammatory potential. Gingerols found in the essential oil and shogaols found in the oleoresin and CO_2 extract inhibit the activation of several genes involved in the inflammatory response. Gingerols can also inhibit the synthesis of inflammation mediators such as prostaglandins and leukotrienes.[34]

Safety

Ginger's toxic rating is I. (ACHS.edu Toxic Rating: I = Low, II = Moderate, III = High (Low Therapeutic Margin).

A skin patch test is recommended for anyone with sensitive skin as it may cause irritation. This usually occurs when applied at full strength, which is not recommended. There have been reports of insignificant potential photosensitivity. However, for anyone with sun sensitivity, exercise caution.

Ginger essential oil, oleoresin, or CO2 extract should not be used for morning sickness or during any stage of pregnancy; and as a precaution, it is advisable to avoid using powdered root capsules. As a food, ginger can be used during pregnancy in normal amounts.

Formulas

Anti-Nausea Calming Blend

Camellia oil is non-greasy and absorbs quickly, but sweet almond or grapeseed oil can also be used.

4 drops Ginger essential oil *Zingiber officinale*
7 drops Bergamot essential oil *Citrus aurantium* var. *bergamia*
10 drops Lavender essential oil *Lavandula angustifolia*
4 drops Peppermint essential oil *Mentha piperita*
30 ml Camellia oil *Camellia sinensis*

In a glass vial or small bottle, blend the essential oils. Add ten drops of the blend to 30 ml of camellia oil. Apply to earlobes, the base of the neck, and the inside of wrists. You can also put the blend into a personal inhaler tube.

Joint Ease Blend

4 drops Ginger essential oil *Zingiber officinale*
10 drops Lavender essential oil *Lavandula angustifolia*
8 drops Peppermint essential oil *Mentha piperita*
8 drops Rosemary essential oil *Rosmarinus officinalis*
1/4 ounce Arnica infused oil *Arnica montana*
1 cup peanut oil (or other base oil, such as sweet almond or grapeseed)

Blend the ginger, lavender, peppermint, and rosemary essential oils with the arnica infused oil; add to peanut or other base oil in a glass jar or bottle. Massage joints frequently with the oil formula.

The essential oil made from fresh ginger rhizomes is very different, with a more complex profile, then that made from dried rhizomes. Both are wonderfully warming, gently stimulating, and have many therapeutic uses.

Susan Belsinger

References

1. Dafni, A., Aqil Khatib, S., & Benítez, G. (2021). "The Doctrine of Signatures in Israel-Revision and Spatiotemporal Patterns." *Plants* (Basel, Switzerland), 10(7), 1346. https://pubmed.ncbi.nlm.nih.gov/. Accessed 9-9-22.

2. Supplement to earlier monographs on Fragrance Raw Materials. (1979). "Monographs on Fragrance Raw Materials." 8–10. https://doi.org/10.1016/b978-0-08-023775-6.50011-4. Accessed 9-9-22.

3. Ibid

4. CFR - Code of Federal Regulations Title 21. accessdata.fda.gov. (n.d.). https://www.accessdata.fda.gov/scripts/cdrh/cfdocs/cfcfr/CFRSearch.cfm?fr=182.20. Accessed 9-1-22.

5. Zhang, L., Pan, C., Ou, Z., Liang, X., Shi, Y., Chi, L., Zhang, Z., Zheng, X., Li, C., & Xiang, H. (2020). "Chemical profiling and bioactivity of essential oils from *Alpinia officinarum* Hance from ten localities in China." *Industrial Crops and Products*, 153, 112583. https://doi.org/10.1016/j.indcrop.2020.112583. Accessed 9-9-22.

6. © ISO. The material is reproduced from ISO 16928:2014 permission of the American National Standards Institute (ANSI) on behalf of the International Organization for Standardization. All rights reserved.

7. Ibid

8. Athavale, A., Athavale, T., & Roberts, D. M. (2020). "Antiemetic drugs: what to prescribe and when." *Australian prescriber*, 43(2), 49–56. https://doi.org/10.18773/austprescr.2020.011. Accessed 9-8-22.

9. Geiger, J. (2005). "The essential oil of ginger and anaesthesia." *International Journal of Aromatherapy*, 15(1), 7-14. https://doi.org/10.1016/j.ijat.2004.12.002.

10. Hunt, R., Dienemann, J., Norton, H.J., Hartley, W., Hudgens, A., Stern, T., et al. (2012). "Aromatherapy as

Treatment for Postoperative Nausea: A Randomized Trial." *Anesthesia & Analgesia,* 117(3), 597–604. https://doi.org/10.1213/ANE.0b013e31824a0b1c. Accessed 9-9-23.

11. Hunt, R., Dienemann, J., Norton, H. J., Hartley, W., Hudgens, A., Stern, T., & Divine, G. (2013). "Aromatherapy as treatment for postoperative nausea: a randomized trial." *Anesthesia and Analgesia,* 117(3), 597–604. https://doi.org/10.1213/ANE.0b013e31824a0b1c. Accessed 9-9-23.

12. Karaman, S., Karaman, T., Tapar, H., Dogru, S., & Suren, M. (2019). "A randomized placebo-controlled study of aromatherapy for the treatment of postoperative nausea and vomiting." *Complementary Therapies in Medicine,* 42, 417–421. https://doi.org/10.1016/j.ctim.2018.12.019. Accessed 9-9-23.

13. Toniolo, J., Delaide, V., & Beloni, P. (2021). "Effectiveness of inhaled aromatherapy on chemotherapy-induced nausea and vomiting: A systematic review." *The Journal of Alternative and Complementary Medicine,* 27(12), 1ute058–1069. https://doi.org/10.1089/acm.2021.0067. Accessed 9-2-23.

14. Williams, A. S., Dove, J., Krock, J. E., Strauss, C. M., Panda, S., Sinnott, L. T., & Rettig, A. E. (2022). "Efficacy of Inhaled Essential Oil Use on Selected Symptoms Affecting Quality of Life in Patients With Cancer Receiving Infusion Therapies." *Oncology nursing forum,* 49(4), 349–358. https://doi.org/10.1188/22.ONF.349-358. Accessed 9-9-23.

15. Williams, A. S., Dove, J., Krock, J. E., Strauss, C. M., Panda, S., Sinnott, L. T., & Rettig, A. E. (2022). "Efficacy of Inhaled Essential Oil Use on Selected Symptoms Affecting Quality of Life in Patients With Cancer Receiving Infusion Therapies." *Oncology nursing forum,* 49(4), 349–358. https://doi.org/10.1188/22.ONF.349-358. Accessed 9-9-23.

16. Saneei Totmaj, A., Emamat, H., Jarrahi, F., & Zarrati, M. (2019). "The effect of Ginger (*Zingiber officinale*) on chemo-

therapy-induced nausea and vomiting in breast cancer patients: A systematic literature review of randomized controlled trials." *Phytotherapy Research*, 33(8), 1957–1965. https://doi.org/10.1002/ptr.6377. Accessed 9-9-23.

17. Ibid

18. Ryan, J. L., Heckler, C. E., Roscoe, J. A., Dakhil, S. R., Kirshner, J., Flynn, P. J., Morrow, G. R. (2012). "Ginger (*Zingiber officinale*) reduces acute chemotherapy-induced nausea: A URCC CCOP study of 576 patients." *Supportive Care in Cancer*, 20(7), 1479–1489. https://doi.org/ 10.1007/s00520-011-1236-3. Accessed 9-9-23.

19. Evans, A., Malvar, J., Garretson, C., Pedroja Kolovos, E., & Baron Nelson, M. (2018). "The Use of Aromatherapy to Reduce Chemotherapy-Induced Nausea in Children With Cancer: A Randomized, Double-Blind, Placebo-Controlled Trial." *Journal of Pediatric Oncology Nursing : Official Journal of the Association of Pediatric Oncology Nurses*, 35(6), 392–398. https://doi.org/10.1177/1043454218782133. Accessed 9-14-23.

20. Khiewkhern, S., Promthet, S., Sukprasert, A., Eunhpinitpong, W., & Bradshaw, P. (2013). "Effectiveness of aromatherapy with light thai massage for cellular immunity improvement in colorectal cancer patients receiving chemotherapy." *Asian Pacific Journal of Cancer Prevention: APJCP*, 14(6), 3903–3907. https://doi.org/10.7314/apjcp.2013.14.6.3903. Accessed 9-24-23.

21. World Health Organization. (n.d.). "Covid-19 pandemic triggers 25% increase in prevalence of anxiety and depression worldwide." *World Health Organization.* https://www.who.int/news/item/02-03-2022-covid-19-pandemic-triggers-25-increase-in-prevalence-of-anxiety-and-depression-worldwide. Accessed 9-15-23.

22. Gao, Y., Bagheri, N., & Furuya-Kanamori, L. (2022, March 29). "Has the COVID-19 pandemic lockdown worsened eating disorders symptoms among patients with eating disorders?

A systematic review." *Zeitschrift fur Gesundheitswissenschaften* = *Journal of Public Health*. https://www.ncbi.nlm.nih.gov/pmc/articles/PMC8961480/. Accessed 9-15-23.

23. Thomas, J. J., Wons, O. B., & Eddy, K. T. (2018). "Cognitive-behavioral treatment of avoidant/restrictive food intake disorder." *Current Opinion in Psychiatry*, 31(6), 425–430. https://doi.org/10.1097/YCO.0000000000000454. Accessed 9-15-23.

24. Burton Murray, H., Jehangir, A., Silvernale, C. J., Kuo, B., & Parkman, H. P. (2020). "Avoidant/restrictive food intake disorder symptoms are frequent in patients antibacterial activity of essential oils from some Philippine plants." *Acta Manilana*, 43:19-23.

25. Ontengco, D.C., Dayap, L.A., & Capal, T.V. (1995). "Screening for the presenting for symptoms of gastroparesis." *Neurogastroenterology & Motility*, 32(12). https://doi.org/10.1111/nmo.13931. Accessed 9-15-23.

26. Squinca, P., Berglund, L., Hanna, K., Rakar, J., Junker, J., Khalaf, H., Farinas, C. S., & Oksman, K. (2021). "Multifunctional Ginger Nanofiber Hydrogels with Tunable Absorption: The Potential for Advanced Wound Dressing Applications." *Biomacromolecules*, 22(8), 3202–3215. https://doi.org/10.1021/acs.biomac.1c00215

27. Quach, H., Le, T. V., Nguyen, T. T., Nguyen, P., Nguyen, C. K., & Dang, L. H. (2022). "Nano-Lipids Based on Ginger Oil and Lecithin as a Potential Drug Delivery System." *Pharmaceutics*, 14(8), 1654. https://doi.org/10.3390/pharmaceutics14081654. Accessed 9-15-23.

28. Wang, X., Shen, Y., Thakur, K., Han, J., Zhang, J. G., Hu, F., & Wei, Z. J. (2020). "Antibacterial Activity and Mechanism of Ginger Essential Oil against Escherichia coli and Staphylococcus aureus." *Molecules* (Basel, Switzerland), 25(17), 3955. https://doi.org/10.3390/molecules25173955. Accessed 9-15-23.

29. Wang, X., Shen, Y., Thakur, K., Han, J., Zhang, J. G., Hu, F., & Wei, Z. J. (2020). "Antibacterial Activity and Mechanism of Ginger Essential Oil against Escherichia coli and Staphylococcus aureus." *Molecules*, (Basel, Switzerland), 25(17), 3955. https://doi.org/10.3390/molecules25173955. Accessed 9-15-23.

30. Singh, G., Kapoor, I. P., Singh, P., de Heluani, C. S., de Lampasona, M. P., & Catalan, C. A. (2008). "Chemistry, antioxidant and antimicrobial investigations on essential oil and oleoresins of *Zingiber officinale*." *Food and Chemical Toxicology: an International Journal Published for the British Industrial Biological Research Association*, 46(10), 3295–3302. https://doi.org/10.1016/j.fct.2008.07.017. Accessed 9-15-23.

31. Gupta, A. K., Baran, R., & Summerbell, R. C. (2000). "Fusarium infections of the skin." *Current Opinion in Infectious Diseases*, 13(2), 121–128. https://doi.org/10.1097/00001432-200004000-00005. Accessed 9-15-23.

32. Pozzatti, P., Scheid, L.A., Spader, T.B., Atayde, M.L., Santurio, J.M., & Alves, S.H. (2008). "In vitro activity of essential oils extracted from plants used as spices against fluconazole-resistant and fluconazole-susceptible Candida spp." *Can J Microbiol*, 54(11):950-6.

33. Tiwari, R., Dikshit, R.P., Chandan, N.C., Saxena, A., Gupta, K.G., & Vadehra D.E. (1983). "Inhibition of Growth and Aflatoxin B1 Production of Aspergillus Parasiticus by Spice Oils." *J Fd Sci Technol*, 20:131-132.

34. Ramadan, G., Al-Kahtani, M. A., & El-Sayed, W. M. (2011). "Anti-inflammatory and antioxidant properties of *Curcuma longa* (turmeric) versus *Zingiber officinale* (ginger) rhizomes in rat adjuvant-induced arthritis." *Inflammation*, 34(4), 291–301. https://doi.org/10.1007/s10753-010-9278-0. Accessed 9-15-23.

Dorene Petersen BA, DIP.NT, DIP.ACU, RH (AHG) is a New Zealand-trained Naturopath and aromatherapy, herbalism, and holistic wellness expert with decades of experience. She founded the American College of Healthcare Sciences (ACHS) in 1978. During that time, she authored twenty textbooks, amongst many other things, and continues to write. Her most immense joy is celebrating successful ACHS students and graduates and sharing wellness tips. She is now retired as the Founding President of the College. Contact Dorene at dorenepetersen@achs.edu.

Ginger rhizome.
Gail Wood Miller

GINGER ~ EAT YOUR MEDICINE

Carol Little

Ginger root is a warming herb, which can raise immunity and nourish the body in so many ways. It can simultaneously soothe our nerves and energize us. I use it in herbal formulae to help move the medicine throughout the body faster. Ginger also helps us to release toxins and can be both building and detoxifying. Ginger medicine has an important place in my herbal apothecary and winter medicine chest.

Ginger is a powerhouse herb. Here are its many attributes*: Analgesic, anthelmintic, antiallergenic, antibacterial, anticonvulsant, antidepressant, antiemetic, antifungal, antimigraine, anti-inflammatory, antispasmodic, antithrombotic, appetite stimulant, blood pressure normalizer, cardiac, carminative, cholagogue, circulatory stimulant, decongestant, diaphoretic, digestive stimulant, diuretic, emmenagogue, expectorant, febrifuge, hepatoprotective, hypocholesterolemic, hypoglycemic, hypolipidemic, immune stimulant, nervine (stimulating), rubefacient, sialogogue, stomachic, and uterine stimulant.

Ginger is anti-nausea and calms motion sickness; ginger with raspberry leaf helps relieve morning sickness. It is an excellent digestive, supporting digestion and calming an upset tummy. It has often been called "Nature's Antacid", as it can help relieve symptoms of acid indigestion.

Ginger is anti-inflammatory overall. In the digestive system, it is supportive for IBS. It is a circulatory herb that can help with poor circulation and heart conditions. Ginger is analgesic so it can help with pain relief.

Experience tells us that drinking ginger tea daily can help to reduce sugar cravings. A therapeutic dose of 3 to 4 cups throughout the day can truly make a difference. Use ginger in the 5 to 10% range in formulas and as a catalyst to support and move other herbs in the body.

Ginger is a special herb at my house. It's also a wonderful example of the idea of using food as medicine. I have some favourite ways to enjoy and use it all year round but tend to start making these concoctions in the fall to be ready with excellent medicinal food throughout the long winter.

Whichever way you choose to use ginger in your own life, I hope you'll try some of these ideas and find your own ways to love and benefit from this amazing herbal ally.

Ginger Infusion

Probably the easiest remedy to prepare, and although simple, ginger tea is an effective remedy for so many ailments. For an even simpler version of this recipe, slice 2 coins of ginger root and toss into your mug. This is quick and tasty, but I admit that I prefer to grate the ginger when time permits, as I find it gives a better digestive result.

Always use organic ingredients whenever possible.

Yields 1 cup

> Fresh ginger root
> Lemon
> Water (good quality pure)
> Raw honey (local when possible)

Grate a small piece of ginger (1 to 2 inches) into a mug. Add the juice of 1/2 lemon. Fill the mug with boiling water. Stir in a teaspoon of honey. Cover and steep for about 5 minutes.

Ginger Syrup

I love to make this special healing syrup. It's easy to make and delightful to give and receive. Ginger syrup is a welcome gift, so make lots to give, and your friends will smile!

Yields about 1 cup

> 1 cup raw honey
> 1 1/2 cups pure water
> 6 ounces ginger root, sliced thin into coins

Combine the honey and the water in a pot and bring to a simmer. Add the ginger. Simmer uncovered for about 45 minutes.

Remove from the heat and strain the ginger out. Allow to cool.

Pour into a clean jar or bottle and label. Store in the fridge. Enjoy within 6 months.

Jazzed-Up Ginger Juice

It has been said that, if we attack a cold/flu with the right remedy at the very beginning, and if we take enough of it, and keep taking it for a couple of days after symptoms subside, we can avert the cold/flu altogether. One such remedy is a concoction I call "Jazzed-up Ginger Juice." It does require a little more time, but when we have all the ingredients on hand, it can be made and ready to use in minutes.

To make the ginger juice, use 2 pounds of good quality organic fresh ginger root. Wash and peel, chop into chunks. Add to juicer (such as a Vitamix) or sturdy blender with 1 cup of water, process. Add 1 cup warm water, strain the pulp through a sieve lined with cheesecloth into a bowl. Squeeze to extract more juice. Pour juice into measuring cup; compost the pulp (Or, it could be decocted, as it still contains beneficial qualities.) Use 4 ounces in recipe; store the remainder in the refrigerator and use within 1 week.

Yields 2 to 2 1/2 cups

  4 ounces fresh ginger juice
  1 tablespoon raw honey
  1/4 cup fresh lime juice
  1/8 teaspoon cayenne powder
  6 ounces good-quality, room-temperature water

Combine the ingredients in a glass jar, mix well and cap. Pour some into a small glass and sip throughout the day.

Ginger-Turmeric Decoction

This is a delicious beverage using ginger and turmeric, which can be very beneficial for easing arthritis or inflammation. The combination is quite tasty; a good daily tonic as a home remedy for overall well-being. This recipe can be altered to suit individual tastes. I like it just like this; and countless clients over the years have proclaimed the anti-inflammatory results to be noticeable, in time.

1 serving

2 cups good-quality water
1/2 teaspoon powdered or 1-inch piece fresh ginger
1/2 teaspoon powdered or 1-inch piece fresh turmeric
1 tablespoon maple syrup
Juice of 1/2 lemon

Bring water to a boil, then add the herbs. Simmer for 10 minutes. Strain decoction into a mug; add maple syrup and lemon juice, stir to combine. Drink warm.

Ginger and turmeric rhizomes.
Susan Belsinger

Ginger Honey

Ginger honey is easy to make and such a helpful herbal remedy to have on hand. Infusing herbs in honey preserves an herb's healing qualities. Herbal-infused honey offers the benefit of the honey plus the healing attributes of the herb being used.

I prefer to use local raw honey whenever possible, which is anti-bacterial, anti-fungal and anti-viral. It's a powerful antioxidant and can strengthen the immune system. Raw honey is an alkaline-producing food which contains its own powerhouse of enzymes, vitamins and nutrients. Raw honey from a local beekeeper is renowned to help in the treatment of seasonal allergies. As a natural expectorant and anti-inflammatory, raw honey is beneficial for respiratory issues like asthma and bronchitis.

Ginger root infused in honey makes a tasty soothing treat for a sore throat, colds and flu. It is an effective herbal remedy for indigestion, flatulence, general stomach cramping, or menstrual discomfort. The anti-inflammatory qualities of ginger marry well with the same qualities in raw honey and produce a helpful remedy for inflammation in general. I've used it with success as part of a treatment protocol for arthritis, tendonitis, and bronchitis. The warming nature of the Ginger Honey helps to stimulate our circulatory system. It can ease the discomfort of cold hands and feet and help to prevent internal blood clots.

2 3-inch pieces of ginger root, sliced into coins
2 lemons, sliced, optional
Raw honey, enough to cover

Place the ginger (and lemon slices, if using) into a glass canning jar. Add the honey slowly. With a chopstick or other non-metal object, gently push the contents down, to allow air bubbles to rise and the honey to completely fill the jar. Close the jar and add the lid, label with date.

The mixture will form a loose syrup. Allow the mixture to sit overnight if possible. Remove the lemons, if used.

Take by the spoonful often to help to soothe your cough or sore throat. Enjoy warm on its own or added to an herbal tea for additional healing power.

Herb-infused honey will last indefinitely, as long as the herb is submerged in the honey. Store in a cool, dark cupboard for up to one year.

References

*The comprehensive list of attributes is from class notes from The Living Earth School of Herbalism directed by Michael Vertolli R.H. https://www.livingearthschool.ca

Carol Little, *R.H. is a traditional herbalist in Toronto, Canada, where she has had a private practice for the last 20+ years. She loves to write about how we can embrace herbs in our daily lives. Her easy-to-digest weekly blog posts offer quick takeaway ideas to help readers to feel their best.*

Carol is a current professional and past board member of the Ontario Herbalists Association. She combines her love of travel and passion for all things green and loves to write about both. Carol has written for Vitality Magazine for many years. She is a regular contributor to the IHA annual Herb of the Year book. She is a proud participant in the recently published FIRE CIDER 101 Zesty Recipes for Health-Boosting Remedies by Rosemary Gladstar and friends.

Carol's current project is a fun-filled "deep dive" into ONE herb each month ~ it's called HerbGals and it's a creative inter-active way to learn about the many gifts and practical ways we can embrace the green world! Herb enthusiasts, herbalists, gardeners or culinary interests? It's about sharing and learning from each other!

https://studiobotanica.teachable.com/p/herbgals; https://www.face-book.com/studiobotanica and https://instagram.com/studiobotanica

Freshly washed ginger rhizomes are recipe-ready.
Susan Belsinger

Ginger Oatmeal Bath Bomb ingredients for a detoxifying, cleansing, and soothing bath.

Janice Cox

NATURAL BEAUTY WITH GINGER

Janice Cox

Enhance your natural beauty and give your skin a healthy glow with ginger. Ginger is one of the oldest spice plants used throughout the world. The fresh roots or rhizomes are easily grown, stored, and transported. For this reason, ginger has been an important and useful plant for over five thousand years. The fresh rhizomes can be stored in your freezer, or dried and ground into a fine powder. Keep dried ginger in a cool, dry, dark spot for the longest shelf life. When it comes to skin and hair care, ginger is used as a "warming" ingredient that helps boost circulation and blood flow. It gives a sweet spicy scent to home-made body care products. Here are some easy recipes for you to create yourself at home.

Fresh Ginger Facial Toner

This is a light and refreshing toner that will give your complexion a healthy glow. Perfect to use after cleansing to reset our skin's natural pH level and help reduce inflammation. It also makes a nice after-bath splash for an energizing start to your day.

Yields 4 ounces

> 1-inch slice fresh ginger root
> 1/2 cup pure water
> 1/8 teaspoon vegetable glycerin or vitamin E oil
> 1 to 2 tablespoons witch-hazel extract

Place the ginger root slice in a small bowl. Heat the water to just boiling and pour over the ginger. Let the mixture steep until cool. Remove the ginger and stir in the remaining ingredients. Pour into a clean container.

To use, splash or spray onto just-washed skin, no need to rinse.

Ginger Hair Oil

This treatment is very effective in stimulating hair growth. It also helps alleviate dandruff and boosts your scalp's circulation. I would not recommend this oil for sensitive skin types because the ginger is spicy and may irritate. This recipe will leave your hair smelling faintly of ginger.

Yields 2 ounces

> 1 teaspoon grated fresh ginger root
> 1/4 cup light oil such as almond, jojoba, or sesame

Place the grated ginger inside a piece of cheesecloth and gently squeeze 1/4 teaspoon of juice into the oil. Mix the oil and juice together with a small spoon or whisk until well blended.

To use, massage the oil into your scalp and leave on for 10 minutes before shampooing. This oil may also be left on the head as a pack treatment, but if your scalp is irritated by the ginger, wash your hair at once and reduce the amount of ginger used.

Ginger Mouth Freshener

You may be familiar with chewing on a sprig of parsley to freshen your breath and aid digestion after a heavy meal; fresh ginger root may be used in much the same manner. Ginger is an effective natural mouth freshener and sugar free.

Lemon Ginger Body Scrub

Body scrubs are beneficial to skin and health because they deep cleanse and boost circulation. This simple scrub will give your skin a healthy glow and energize your whole body. If you are applying in the shower, make sure you stand on a non-skid mat or bath towel, as the oil can make things a bit slippery.

Yields 10 ounces

1 cup raw or coconut sugar
2 tablespoons finely grated fresh ginger root
1/4 cup light oil such as jojoba, grape seed, or olive oil
1 teaspoon grated lemon zest

In a bowl mix together all ingredients and spoon into a clean container with a tight-fitting lid.

To use, in the tub or shower massage in circular motions into damp skin with a cotton washcloth or your hands. Be careful around sensitive skin areas. Rinse off and pat skin dry.

Gingerbread Bath Mix

If you like baking gingerbread cookies and houses, then this is the bath mixture for you. Full of sugar and spice, this bath mix will help you relax and refresh. The natural spices and ginger have antiseptic and stimulating properties. They will help boost your circulation and cleanse toxins from your body. The baking soda in the mixture soothes sore muscles and cleanses your skin.

Yields 5 ounces

- 1 teaspoon ground (or freshly ground dried) cinnamon
- 1 teaspoon ground (or freshly ground dried) ginger
- 1/2 teaspoon ground (or freshly ground dried) clove buds
- 1/2 cup baking soda
- 2 tablespoons raw or granulated sugar

Grind together the cinnamon, ginger, and clove buds in a food processor or clean coffee grinder.

Place all ingredients in a bowl and stir well to combine. Pour into a clean jar or decorative container.

To use, add 1/4 cup to a warm bath and soak for 20 minutes to relax your muscles.

Ginger Oatmeal Bath Bomb

If you were to do an internet search about using ginger in the bath, you will find a long list of benefits from boosting energy to relieving anxiety. Ginger is a powerful detox ingredient because it increases your circulation and allows your body to rid itself of toxins. A ginger bath is very relaxing and the perfect way to end a busy day. These bombs also contain ground oatmeal, which many people use in place of soap. Oatmeal is effective in the bath, as it calms your skin and is naturally cleansing and soothing.

Yields 16 ounces, about 6 bombs

    1 cup baking soda
    1 cup citric acid powder
    1/4 cup finely ground whole oats
    1 tablespoon powdered ginger
    1/4 cup Epsom salts
    1/2 cup coconut oil, melted

In a large bowl, mix together baking soda, citric acid power, oats, ginger, and Epsom salts. Melt the coconut oil in the microwave or on the stovetop. You may add some essential oils to the melted oil for scent.

Slowly add to the dry ingredients and mix well; you will have a mixture that looks like wet sand. Mix well with a small spoon or fork. Then pack the mixture tightly in a mold – you can use bath bomb molds, muffin tins, or ice cube trays to create your bath bombs or tablets. Let the mixture sit until firm then unmold onto a cookie sheet and allow to dry overnight.

To use, drop in a tub full of warm water and enjoy

Note: If you make smaller-sized bath bombs these can be used in foot and hand baths.

Fresh Ginger Root Bath

Fresh ginger root has a sweet, spicy fragrance that is also a mild stimulant. Used in the bath, it promotes circulation and is perfect on a cold winter day to warm both your body and your senses. In addition, place a few fresh slices along with some lemon slices in a cup of hot water, to enjoy as a tea while in the bath. Ginger is a natural detox and makes a refreshing caffeine-free tea.

Yields 8 ounces, enough for one bath

1/2 cup baking soda
2 tablespoons freshly grated ginger root (or 1 tablespoon dried)
1/2 cup water

Mix together all the ingredients and pour into a clean container.

To use, pour the entire mixture into the bath as you fill the tub, stir well, and soak for 15 to 20 minutes. After bathing, dress warmly, as this bath is super cleansing and really opens up all of your pores. It is best done in the evening before going to sleep.

Japanese Spice Bath

The bath is a daily ritual in Japan. The bathtub is entered after the body is thoroughly washed and rinsed. The Japanese bathe to purify themselves and soothe both the body and mind. The home bath is taken in solitude and is time to center oneself. This is opposed to communal bathing, where conversation and the company of others is enjoyed. Natural ingredients, such as flowers, fruits, and spices, are added to the hot bathwater for medicinal, symbolic, and body-beautifying reasons.

This bath contains Asian spices, fresh ginger root, and pine that add a pleasant fragrance to the water and help warm the body.

Yields 8 ounces, enough for one bath

Use about 2 ounces of each:

> Anise seeds
> Ginger root
> Pine needles
> Chrysanthemum flowers

Tie the anise, ginger, and pine needles inside a piece of cheesecloth and hang under your tub's faucet. Fill the tub with very warm water. Float the chrysanthemum flowers on the water. Wash and scrub your body thoroughly, using a shower or faucet separate from your bathtub. Enter your tub and relax, let your mind clear, and try not to think about anything in particular.

When you are done soaking in the tub, rinse or shower one more time with water as cool as you can stand. Towel dry and apply a light bath oil to lock in moisture absorbed in the bath.

Here are some simple ways to use ginger for body care:

Add a fresh slice of ginger to your favorite herbal tea blend to help warm your body and aid digestion.

Give yourself a warming footbath by adding some fresh or dried ginger to a tub of water with 1 cup Epsom salts and 1/2 cup baking soda.

When using henna as a natural hair color, add some dried ginger to the mixture to help reduce the henna scent and boost your scalp's circulation and promote hair growth.

An easy detox bath mix is two tablespoons of dried ginger and 2 cups of baking soda to a hot bath in the evening before bedtime.

Janice Cox is an expert on the topic of natural beauty and making your own cosmetic products with simple kitchen and garden ingredients. She is the author of six best-selling books on the topic: Natural Beauty at Home, Natural Beauty for All Seasons, Natural Beauty from the Garden, Beautiful Luffa, Beautiful Lavender, and Beautiful Flowers. She was the beauty editor for Herb Quarterly Magazine for over twenty years. Mrs. Cox is a featured speaker at the Mother Earth News Magazine Fairs, Botanical Gardens and Lifestyle events. She is a Regional Director for Garden Communicators International, the Education Chair for The Herb Society of America, and a member of the International Herb Association. She lives in Southern Oregon. Email: Janice@naturalbeautyathome.com. Instagram: athomebeauty; Website: www.naturalbeautyathome.com.

Ginger root tresses.
Janice Cox

BIOS FOR ILLUSTRATORS AND PHOTOGRAPHERS

Susan Belsinger — see bio in "Take a Walk on the Wild Side with the Other Ginger."

Lucie Day — see bio in "Growing Tropical Ginger in Southern Oregon."

Janice Cox — see bio in "Natural Beauty with Ginger."

Karen England — see bio in "Pickled-Back-Cocktail."

Deborah Hall — see bio in "Take a Walk on the Wild Side with the Other Ginger."

Pat Kenny, retired medical illustrator, has been a member of the IHA since it was IHGMA. A member of HSA since 1979 and Vice President of IHA, Pat gives photo-illustrated herb talks and demos, neighborhood-to-nation. She is a supporter of the nation's largest public herb garden, the National Herb Garden in Washington, DC. Pat's first illustration request that was not part of a human's anatomy was a watercolor painting of a violet. She was told by her father that the first time she tried to run away at the age of four, she was found picking violets in the nearby woods. She's been found in and out of the woods ever since.

Alicia Mann is a classically trained artist and metalsmith at Heritage Metalworks, LTD, in Downington, Pennsylvania. A graduate of Maryland College of Art, she integrates her interests in art and horticulture by growing flowers, herbs, vegetables, and fruit trees. Alicia recently illustrated Bevin Cohen's book, *The Complete Guide to Seed and Nut Oils.*

Cooper Murray — see bio in "Gingerlicious."

Gail Wood Miller coaches, writes, speaks, draws, and does watercolors. She is a retired professor of English and English education, active in educational consulting. She often combines this as certified holistic health coach and ADHD coach, in her research and in her conference presentations. Gail specializes in working with women and children. She is a member of the Philadelphia Sketch Club and the Musconetcong Watercolor Group. She has studied at the Herzfeld School of Art, Cooper Union, the Minerva Foundation for Figure Drawing, and Salmagundi.

Diann Nance — see bio in "Ginger Memories."

Karen O'Brien — see bio in "Zingy Ginger ~ A Spicy History."

Marge Powell — see bio in "Gingers in My Florida Garden."

Tina Marie Wilcox — see bio in "Growing Ginger in the. Ozarks."

COVER CREDITS

Design: Susan Belsinger and Heather Cohen

Front Cover:

Background image and upper left: Susan Belsinger

Lower right: Lucie Day

Back Cover:

Susan Belsinger

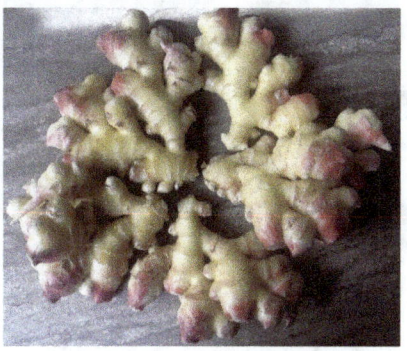

A mandala of fresh ginger rhizomes.
Susan Belsinger

INTERNATIONAL HERB ASSOCIATION'S HERBS OF THE YEAR 1995 THROUGH 2025

1995 Fennel *Foeniculum* spp.

1996 Monarda *Monarda* spp.

1997 Thyme *Thymus* spp.

1998 Mint *Mentha* spp.

1999 Lavender *Lavandula* spp.

2000 Rosemary *Rosmarinus* spp.

2001 Sage *Salvia* spp.

2002 Echinacea *Echinacea* spp.

2003 Basil *Ocimum* spp.

2004 Garlic *Allium sativum*

2005 Oregano *Origanum* spp.

2006 Scented Geranium *Pelargonium* spp.

2007 Lemon Balm *Melissa* spp.

2008 Calendula *Calendula* spp.

2009 Bay Laurel *Laurus* spp.

2010 Dill *Anethum* spp.

2011 Horseradish *Armoracia* spp.

2012 Rose *Rosa* spp.

2013 Elderberry *Sambucus* spp.

2014 Artemisia *Artemisia* spp.

2015 Savory *Satureja* spp.

2016 Capsicum *Capsicum* spp.

2017 Cilantro & Coriander *Coriandrum* spp.

2018 Hops *Humulus* spp.

2019 Anise Hyssop & all others *Agastache* spp.

2020 Raspberry, blackberry, et al. *Rubus* spp.

2021 Parsley *Petroselinum* spp.

2022 Viola *Viola* spp.

2023 Ginger *Zingiber officinale*

2024 Yarrow *Achillea millefolium*

2025 Chamomile *Matricaria* spp. & *Chamaemelum* spp.

Ginger rhizome.
Alicia Mann

Just-harvested ginger rhizomes with leaves.
Susan Belsinger